Bankruptcy

We Wrote the Book on It

(The Real Story and Concerns People Have Based Upon Thousands of Cases Our Lawyers Have Handled)

By Attorney Ronald C. Sykstus*

and

the Bond and Botes team of lawyers

225 Pratt Avenue
Huntsville, Alabama 35801
Offices located in Alabama,
Mississippi, and Tennessee
www.bondandbotes.com

*Admitted to Practice: Alabama; Illinois; Tennessee; Washington, D.C.; U.S. Court of Appeals for Veterans Claims; U.S. Tax Court.

Board Certified in Consumer Bankruptcy Law by the American Board of Certification

First published by Dog Ear Publishing
4010 W. 86th Street, Ste H
Indianapolis, IN 46268
www.dogearpublishing.net

ISBN: 978-1-4575-3621-2

This book is printed on acid-free paper.

Printed in the United States of America

Contents

Chapter 1 Introduction
The Stress and Worry of Debt 7

Chapter 2 Our Lawyers and Affiliated Law Firms 12

Chapter 3 What Happens When a Prospective Client Comes into One of Our Offices? 16

Chapter 4 What Is Bankruptcy? (History and Famous Cases) 19

Chapter 5 Moral Guidance and Thoughts on Debt 34

Chapter 6 Getting Started With Us (How to Get Your Credit Reports) 40

Chapter 7 Effect of Bankruptcy on a Credit Report and How to Improve a Credit Report After a Bankruptcy Filing 44

Chapter 8 Should I Use a Debt Management Company or a Debt Relief Company to Handle My Debts? 49

Chapter 9 Do I Lose Everything I Own When I File for Bankruptcy and What Property Can I Protect? 56

Chapter 10 Time Limits Between Bankruptcy Filings 70

Chapter 11 Should I File for Bankruptcy? If So, What Type Should I File and How Can It Help Me? 74

Chapter 12 Bankruptcy Concepts and Issues 80

A. Credit Counseling and Financial Management/Debtor Education Requirements 80

B. What Happens at a Meeting with a Bankruptcy Attorney? 81

C. The Automatic Stay 82

D. If I Am Considering Filing for Bankruptcy and I Am Married, Am I Required to File Bankruptcy with My Spouse? 84

E. What Is a Bankruptcy Trustee? 85

F. Can I Be Denied a Bankruptcy Discharge from My Debts? 86

G. Can I Be Held Responsible for Another Person's Debts Like My Husband/Wife/Parent/Child/Friend? 87

H. How Will Bankruptcy Affect My Bank Account? 87

I. What Is the Presumption of Abuse in a Chapter 7 Bankruptcy? 89

J. Can I Dismiss My Chapter 7 Bankruptcy If I Change My Mind After Filing? 90

K. What Is a Chapter 13 Plan? 91

L. What Is the Best Interest in Bankruptcy? 93

M. Can I File Bankruptcy If I Am Unemployed? 94

N. Are Co-Debtors Protected If I File for Bankruptcy? 95

O. Can a School Withhold My Transcripts If I Included My School Tuition in My Bankruptcy? 96

P. What Is a 341 Meeting of Creditors? 97

Q. Will I Continue to Pay Interest to My Creditors That I Include in My Chapter 13 Bankruptcy? 98

R. How Long Can I Stay in My House If I Am Giving It up in Bankruptcy? 99

S. If I Am Surrendering My House in Bankruptcy, How Should I Go About It? 100

T. How Soon After Chapter 7 Bankruptcy Can You Buy a New House? 101

U. How Long Can I Keep My Car After Filing Chapter 7 Straight Bankruptcy? 103

V. What Is a Reaffirmation Agreement in Bankruptcy? 104

W. How Soon After Chapter 7 Bankruptcy Can You Buy a New Car? 105

X. How Will Filing for Bankruptcy Affect My Government Security Clearance? 106

Y. Payday Advance Issues and Bankruptcy 107

Z. Can You File Bankruptcy on a Timeshare? 111

Chapter 13 What Should I do If I Am Sued? How to Defend a Lawsuit and the Potential Consequences If You Do Not 112

Chapter 14 Divorce and Bankruptcy 127

Chapter 15 Taxes and Bankruptcy 131

Chapter 16 Student Loans and Bankruptcy 138

Chapter 17 Business Bankruptcy – Chapter 11 143

Chapter 18 Family Farmer and Family Fisherman Reorganization – Chapter 12 145

Chapter 19 Miscellaneous Consumer Laws That Everyone Should Know 150

A. Fair Debt Collection Practices Act (FDCPA) 150

B. Fair Credit Reporting Act (FCRA) 152

C. Telephone Consumer Protection Act (TCPA) 155

D. Credit Repair Organization Act (CROA) 157

E. Electronic Funds Transfer Act (EFTA) 159

F. Fair Credit Billing Act (FCBA) 160

Chapter 20 Conclusion 162

Chapter 1

Introduction
The Stress and Worry of Debt

We are often asked what our clients are like. Are they young or old? Are they Caucasian, African-American, Hispanic, or Asian? Are they married or single? What kind of jobs do they have? Are they lawyers, doctors, dentists, engineers, cashiers, teachers, construction workers, or waitresses? Are some of them unemployed? Do they own homes, beach homes, vacation homes, or office buildings? Are they 18 years old? Are they 25 years old? Are they 35 years old? Are they 45 years old? Are they 55 years old? Are they 65 years old? Are they 75 years old? Are they 85 years old? Do they have high school degrees? Do they have college degrees? Do they have master's degrees? Do they have professional degrees? Do they have law degrees? Do they have medical degrees? Do they have PhDs? You get the picture. Our clients are all of these people. Debt and the stress of debt does not discriminate. It happens. As the saying goes, unfortunately, bad things sometimes do happen to good people.

Along with being asked what our clients are like, the next question we get usually revolves around some aspect of whether our clients simply run up debt and then gleefully look for ways to get around paying back the debt. That is absolutely and patently false. In the almost 25 years of our law practice, we have encountered very few individuals who willfully ran up debt and then tried to get around paying back the debt. Needless to say, we declined to represent these people. While not an empirical study, this assessment covers thousands upon thousands of people, all fitting the vast array of people as described above who are our clients. We start with the premise that people want to pay back their debt. The absolute last place they want to be is sitting in one of our offices. We understand that, and that is the approach we take in discussing all issues with our clients. We search for ways for people to work out and pay their debt without doing damage to themselves, if there is any possible way to do that.

Why do people come to our offices? It is really rather simple. The stress and worry of their situation makes them feel like they have no place to turn. Obviously, if someone has no debt issues at all, is completely current on all their bills, and has savings in the bank, then they do not need to see us about debt problems or issues and they may come to us for other reasons such as tax or student loan issues (more on that later). People come to us for financial consultations if they are feeling overwhelmed with their debt situation and believe that they will not be able to make some or all of the payments that are due on next month's bills. They may be getting collection calls from both creditors and/or debt collectors to their home, work, or cell phone numbers. They may be receiving threatening collection letters from creditors and debt collectors. They may be served with a lawsuit by the county sheriff or in the mail. They may receive a garnishment of their wages. The IRS or state taxing authorities may be threatening a levy of their wages. They may be being threatened with an automobile repossession by their car creditor. Their mortgage company may be threatening to foreclose on their home or, worse, a foreclosure action may already have been started.

One of the above is usually the start point for us with any prospective new client that comes to our office. Our system and philosophy are pretty simple at this point. No one knows their own individual debt situation like every one of our unique clients. We ask our prospective clients to come into our office for a free consultation visit. We ask them to fill out a simple information form, and we address their debt situation with them privately, confidentially, and, most importantly, in a dignified, respectful manner and without judgment. Anyone who says he or she is a stranger to worry about debt, financial stress, and money issues is either delusional, a liar, or a family member of Bill Gates or Warren Buffet. Other than those two last examples, all of us, at one time or another in our lives, have experienced the stress that the overwhelming majority of people who come to our offices feel and express to us. We understand the worry and the pressure and we want to help people deal with the stress in the calmest, most rational and sensible way possible. We like to move slowly with our clients and let them tell us what results they want to see and what exact worries they have that they want alleviated. The mission statement that our lawyers and affiliated law offices follow and, incidentally, believe in wholeheartedly is this: Our clients are like our family members and friends, and we view the relationship we have with our clients in that way. Our legal practice centers around treating all of our clients with dignity, respect, and compassion while providing the most professional, caring, and expeditious legal counsel and representation that we possibly can. We care and we are ready to help you if you need us.

In reading this, it may seem like we are touting ourselves as the greatest thing since sliced bread. I hope it doesn't appear that way. I hope what is expressed here is that all of our lawyers and staff earnestly and eagerly try to follow the golden rule: Treat others exactly as you want to be treated yourself. Since we have worked hard to get to the jobs we have (and are fortunate enough to have jobs!), why wouldn't we do our absolute best to take the absolute best care of our clients? They are the people who allow us to have jobs. No one wants to come to our offices. We understand that. However, if someone does have to come to us, for any reason, we want it to be the best possible encounter with a lawyer and law firm as possible, under the circumstances. We pride ourselves on customer service and care – lawyers already have a bad enough reputation. We hope to change that perception as much as we can! We like to think that maybe our philosophy is one of the reasons we have been a growing and respected law firm for the past two decades.

One last item before we move on. This is not a self-help book. There are books out there available for people who want to try to file bankruptcy themselves. This book is not for that purpose. I am not good with handyman type work, as my wife often reminds me. As a result, if I were to try to fix, for instance, a broken wood drawer in our house, in all likelihood, I would spend a lot of time trying to fix it and then still have to contact the handyman to come in and repair not only what was initially broken, but what I further messed up. With the bankruptcy, the consequences of messing up your own individual case can be extremely dire, including everything from being denied the discharge of a certain debt, to being denied your entire bankruptcy discharge and still owing all of your debts, to having to come up with a substantial amount of money to pay the bankruptcy trustee, not to mention possible criminal charges and loss of assets. What we often tell clients who come to see us is if they are attempting to get rid of potentially tens of thousands of dollars' worth of debt, that there are eyes looking over what they submit to the court and there are creditors who are not going to be happy about losing out on money that they believe is owed to them. As a result, wouldn't you want to do it exactly right? To that end, hiring a low-cost petition preparer to do the bankruptcy for you, where they tell you that they are saving you a lot of money over high-priced lawyers, makes no sense as well. Is it worth it to save $500 to $600 when we are talking about discharging or consolidating thousands of dollars? We don't think so. If things go wrong, that $500 to $600 you saved initially doesn't look so good.

Our lawyers have handled thousands and thousands of cases over the past 25 years for all different types of people and situations. We discuss cases among one another, and we utilize our collective experience and knowledge to try and get the best results for our clients. As a result, it is our personal belief that over 150 years of aggregate bankruptcy experience is worth a little extra money for someone trying to get through and around thousands of dollars of debt. Beyond that, we truly want people to go through this process with us and move on with their lives in a dignified and relaxed manner without the stress. We view the people we help as clients for life. We want, however, to help them with other things for which they may need legal help and not with a subsequent bankruptcy filing, if at all possible. It is our belief that our clients should use the bankruptcy filing as a springboard to learn as much as they can and to never be in a situation again where debt controls them, their families, or their finances.

Chapter 2

Our Lawyers and Affiliated Law Firms

Before we begin the substantive stuff, just a little bit about our law practice, lawyers, and affiliated law firms.

The law firm of Bond and Botes, P.C., began in 1989 in Birmingham, Alabama, by two law school friends, Mark Bond and Brad Botes. After practicing initially in general areas of law, Mark and Brad then decided to devote their entire law practice to the area of consumer bankruptcy. Since that time, the law firm has evolved into additional areas of law and has expanded its geographic locations into several states. Currently, the law firm has offices in Alabama, Mississippi, and Tennessee. Each office is owned by other Bond and Botes shareholders, and each office is a separate legal entity with a managing shareholder on the ground. As a result, we refer to these offices as the affiliated law offices of Bond and Botes.

You can read personal biographies about our lawyers at the firm website (www.bondandbotes.com), but I thought I would take a minute to tell you, subjectively, a couple of thoughts I have about each of the lawyers in our firm. It is my personal belief that each of these lawyers is an outstanding legal advocate but, more importantly, they are wonderful, upstanding, and principled individuals who care deeply about their clients and, of course, their families.

Mark Bond is a brilliant businessman who retired from the practice of law in 2006 to tend to his multitude of business ventures. We miss Mark but we are grateful for his entrepreneurial spirit and inquisitive mind, which helped get these law offices started.

Brad Botes practices in our Birmingham office. Brad is our global visionary leader and he guides all of the shareholders, lawyers, and staff. Brad is an absolute fountain of knowledge as it relates to bankruptcy and consumer law. In addition, Brad is the most compassionate person I know, both in his personal and professional life. Brad practices along with Suzanne Shinn and Robert Reese in our Birmingham office. Both Suzanne and Robert are tremendous lawyers, insightful, empathetic, and well recognized as leaders in the field.

Carla Handy manages our Gadsden, Alabama, office. Carla is a recognized leader in the practice of consumer bankruptcy and served as the president of the bankruptcy bar section of the Alabama State Bar in 2013. Carla also has a subspecialty practice in the area of farmer bankruptcy under Chapter 12 of the Bankruptcy Code. She is one of the few lawyers in the state who handles this type of bankruptcy for farmers. Carla's counsel is sought out not only by prospective clients but also by attorneys who seek her guidance for complicated matters.

Grant McNutt manages our Florence and Haleyville, Alabama, offices. His practice area covers the entire Shoals area to include the western division of the state of Alabama in Haleyville and Tuscaloosa, Alabama. Grant is very well regarded throughout the western part of the state and is the epitome of the true Southern gentleman.

Nick Gajewski practices in our Florence and Haleyville offices along with Grant McNutt. Nick is a Phi Beta Kappa and Magna Cum Laude graduate from the University of Alabama. A scholar and a very bright lawyer, Nick has extensive experience in the practice of consumer bankruptcy law.

Gail Donaldson and Mary Pool practice in our offices located in Montgomery and Selma, Alabama. Both are very well regarded in the field of bankruptcy law. As an interesting side note, Gail started as a paralegal in the Montgomery office and went through law school and now manages the Montgomery office. Clearly, she is an individual who knows every nuance of our practice from the ground up.

Cindy Lawson runs our Knoxville, Tennessee, office. She has been practicing in the field of consumer bankruptcy for over fifteen years. Cindy has a tremendous work ethic and, along with being very bright, insightful, and incisive, she is a very caring and empathetic individual.

Ed Woods runs our Mississippi offices. There are not many lawyers in Mississippi better than Ed Woods. He is thoughtful and considerate and has spent many years practicing in this area of the law. Ed is very well regarded throughout the state for his legal ability. Joshua Lawhorn also practices throughout the state of Mississippi with Ed Woods, and he is tenacious, bright, and understanding, and has seen every issue as it relates to consumer bankruptcy.

I practice in our Huntsville and Decatur, Alabama, offices along with Amy Tanner, James Ezzell, and Kathryn Davis. I am fortunate to be surrounded by the great lawyers in our office. Amy Tanner currently serves as the state chair for Alabama for the National Association of Consumer Bankruptcy Attorneys (NACBA). She is a tremendously bright and personable lawyer with a work ethic that is second to none. James Ezzell is a compassionate, smart, and understanding lawyer who heads up our firm's Social Security practice. Attorney Kathryn Davis previously worked for one of the local Chapter 7 bankruptcy trustees, so she has an especially keen understanding of the bankruptcy process. She is bright, incisive, and compassionate along with being a very good attorney.

As I re-read what I've written about these lawyers, I could put down the same words for each one of them. Each of the lawyers in our offices is learned in the areas in which they practice. Obviously, I have a bias, but I would dare say that there are not many better bankruptcy lawyers than these individuals. Each of them brings and carries forth the philosophy started by Mark Bond and Brad Botes, as far as compassion and empathy and a tremendous work ethic, to ensure that they serve their clients in the absolute best way possible. All of us try to then instill those same qualities, values, and outlook in our staff members, as far as trying to bring the ultimate experience to our clients, who come to us at one of the lowest and most stressful points in their lives.

As for me, I was an active-duty U.S. Army JAG officer and attorney prior to joining the Bond and Botes team of lawyers. My law practice is limited to consumer bankruptcy, consumer law, VA disability claims, Social Security disability claims, and security clearance revocation defense.

A number of our offices also practice additional areas of law to include Social Security disability, VA disability, security clearance revocation defense, lawsuit defense, tax issues, student loan problems, FDCPA, and FCRA, among other practice areas. All of us also have a large referral source of lawyers we know very well and in whom we trust implicitly. If a client comes to us and has a case or issue in an area of law in which we do not practice, we will refer our clients personally to one of our trusted colleagues. Our rules for referring a client is to only send them to a lawyer we would use personally (or have used) so that we know exactly the experience that the client we are referring will receive.

Chapter 3

What Happens When a Prospective Client Comes into One of Our Offices?

When a prospective client calls one of our offices to set up an initial consultation appointment for any type of debt matter or issue, we will try to send them our information packet by e-mail if at all possible. If that is not possible, then the prospective client can fill out a simple information form in our office when he or she arrives. The prospective client can also complete the information form online and submit it to us via our website. That information form is located directly at our website, www.bondandbotes.com. Furthermore, as an aid to figuring out a person's exact financial situation, the prospective client can get a **FREE** copy of all of his or her three credit reports from www.annualcreditreport.com. This is the Federal Trade Commission (FTC) mandated website that allows all Americans to get one credit report per 12 months from each of the three main credit reporting agencies: Experian, Equifax, and TransUnion. We always tell our clients, however, to make sure that they are at a working printer the moment they get to their credit reports and both **print** off and save to a hard drive their credit reports as soon as they see them. An individual is only entitled to one look per 12 months from each of the three main credit reporting agencies, so, again, please make sure you are at a working printer when you see your credit reports and **print them immediately as you are viewing them**.

The initial consultation that our affiliated law offices offer with regard to any financial issue is free of charge. There are some other areas of law where we may charge a fee for an initial consultation, but the prospective client is told that prior to arrival. Again, for any issue that relates to or revolves around debt or debt collection, the consultation with one of our lawyers is free of charge and at no initial cost to the prospective client. When the client arrives at our office, they will present our receptionist with either the information form that they were able to receive and print off by email or, if they filled out the information form online and emailed it directly to our website, we will print that for them. If the prospective client was not able to do either of these, then he or she will simply be given the information form to fill out in our lobby upon arrival. This prospective client will then sit down in a private and confidential setting with one of our licensed attorneys to review his or her financial situation. We like to understand our prospective clients' entire financial background to include house payments and loans, car payments and loans, tax debt, student loan debt, credit card debt, payday advance debt, signature loans, medical debt, etc., along with the gross monthly income for the family unit and approximate expenses that the family spends each month. We always tell our prospective clients that the more we know and can learn about their own unique situation in our confidential setting, the better position we are in to counsel them. We will look at the prospective client's entire situation and give them the best possible advice. Many times, that advice is to not file any type of bankruptcy at all and to try a different solution.

Clients need not be worried that they will be unnecessarily steered into any type of bankruptcy through our firm, and we probably push away half of the people who come to see us, and we further advise them of alternative solutions that they should explore. Our advice to anyone who comes to us is to use bankruptcy as a last resort and to exhaust all other options first. We are also pretty adept at helping clients identify some other potential options that they may have available. Our lawyers are also knowledgeable and trained in the areas of divorce as it relates to bankruptcy, and credit as it relates to bankruptcy. As a result, we try to evaluate and explore a prospective client's situation from all angles. Sometimes, prospective clients will call us on the telephone and simply want to discuss their situation over the phone. They may also inquire as to what is the cheapest price we can give them. Doing so would be a disservice to the prospective client. We are not in a position to adequately and competently advise them unless we see and review their entire financial situation with them. Additionally, we always tell our prospective clients that they are not buying something at a flea market, so this is not the time to try to haggle out "the best price" when they are talking about potentially thousands and thousands of dollars that they owe to creditors who want their money and how that will impact them for, literally, the rest of their lives. That is why we are adamant about our prospective clients taking advantage of our free consultation to explore their situation.

When prospective clients come to our office, they will not meet with a paralegal or secretary, but with one of the licensed and knowledgeable attorneys that I have already referenced in this text. We pride ourselves on customer and client service for no other reason than it allows us to sleep very well at night and do the absolute best job possible on behalf of the prospective client. Further, it allows us to live by the golden rule so that we can treat the prospective client exactly as we would like to be treated if we were in the same exact situation.

Chapter 4

What Is Bankruptcy? (History and Famous Cases)

Bankruptcy is a legal status of a person or other entity (a business, corporation, municipality, farmer, etc.) that cannot repay the debts it owes to its creditors. In most jurisdictions, bankruptcy is imposed by a court order, most often initiated by the debtor, which is the name assigned to the person or entity filing the bankruptcy case.

The word *bankruptcy* is derived from Italian *banca rotta*, meaning "broken bench," which may stem from a custom of breaking a moneychanger's bench or counter to signify his insolvency. The word itself dates back to the 1500s.[1]

In Ancient Greece, bankruptcy did not exist. If a man owed debts that he could not pay, he and his wife, children, or servants were forced into "debt slavery" until the creditor recouped losses through their physical labor. This form of debt slavery was limited to a period of five years; debt slaves had protection of life and limb, which regular slaves

---

1 "Online Etymology Dictionary." Online Etymology Dictionary. http://www.etymonline.com/ (accessed July 29, 2014).

did not enjoy. However, servants of the debtor could be retained beyond that deadline by the creditor and were often forced to serve their new lord for a lifetime, usually under significantly harsher conditions.

In the Old Testament, every seventh year is decreed by Mosaic Law as a Sabbatical year wherein the release of all debts that are owed by members of the community, except foreigners, is mandated. The seventh Sabbatical year, or forty-ninth year, is then followed by another Sabbatical year known as the Year of Jubilee wherein the release of all debts is mandated, for fellow community members and foreigners alike, and the release of all debt-slaves is also mandated. The Year of Jubilee is announced in advance on the Day of Atonement or the tenth day of the seventh month in the forty-ninth year by the blowing of trumpets throughout the land of Israel.

The Statute of Bankrupts of 1542 was the first codified law under English law dealing with bankruptcy or insolvency. Bankruptcy is also documented in Asia. A failure of a nation to meet bond repayments has been seen on many occasions. The King of Spain had to declare four state bankruptcies for Spain in 1557, 1560, 1575, and 1596.[2]

The history of bankruptcy in the United States dates back to our founding fathers. Article 1, Section 8, clause 4 of the Constitution gives Congress the power to establish uniform bankruptcy laws in the United States.

> Article 1, Section 8 of the Constitution provides as follows:
>
> The Congress shall have power to lay and collect taxes, duties, imposts and excises, to pay the debts and provide for the common defense and general welfare of the United

---

[2] "History of Bankruptcy." creditwrench.com. http://www.creditwrench.com/newsroom/historyofbankruptcy.html (accessed February 6, 2007).

> States; but all duties imposts and excises shall be uniform throughout the United States;
>
> To borrow money on the credit of the United States;
>
> To regulate commerce with foreign nations, and among the several states and with the Indian tribes;
>
> **To establish a uniform rule of naturalization, and uniform laws on the subject of bankruptcies throughout the United States…**

In 1800, by one vote, Congress passed the first American bankruptcy law. The old bankruptcy law was somewhat harsh and restrictive and, in 1841, Congress passed a revised bankruptcy law after it abolished debtors' prisons. This new act allowed for both merchant and non-merchant debtors. There were limits on what debts could be discharged. Both debtors and creditors were allowed to file cases and, as a result of the allowance of voluntary bankruptcies, thousands of debtors received discharges, and creditors received very little of their debt paid back during this time period. This act was repealed after only two years.

Congress formulated yet another bankruptcy law in 1867. This law allowed for both merchant and non-merchants to file voluntary and involuntary cases. As part of that law, debtors were required to also take an oath of allegiance to the United States since this was just after the Civil War. This law lasted 11 years and was repealed again because too many debtors were accused of abusing it and creditors were getting too little money back in return. It is well settled that modern American bankruptcy had its "official" beginning with the Bankruptcy Act of 1898. This law allowed for both voluntary and involuntary cases; it permitted debtors to claim exemptions and removed most barriers from discharging most debts. This law remained intact and was amended in the 1920s to add specific grounds for the denial of a discharge, and it specifically excepted certain debts from discharge in the bankruptcy filing. In 1938, Congress made another substantive change to the bankruptcy law. Many of the changes in 1938 affected business bankruptcies, but the law also established Chapter 13, the wage earner's repayment plan. It is all referred to as debtor's court and debt consolidation. As an interesting side note, Chapter 13 bankruptcy really had its start in Birmingham, Alabama. Professors Timothy W. Dixon and David G. Epstein wrote a great article published in the ABI Law Review, Volume 10, titled "Where did Chapter 13 come from and where should it go?"[3] In fact, professors Dixon and Epstein noted that "Birmingham, Alabama" is the short answer to the question of where Chapter 13 came from. Mr. Valentine Nesbitt, according to the article, started a form of Chapter 13 which was very successful in Birmingham. Congressman Walter Clift Chandler of Tennessee introduced Chapter 13 in the Chandler Act as a direct result of what he learned of the Birmingham debtor's court success first started by Valentine Nesbitt. It is no wonder, then, that the southern states of Tennessee, Alabama, and Georgia filed a majority of the bankruptcy cases under Chapter 13.

From 1938 until 1978, there were no changes to the bankruptcy law. In 1978, Congress enacted the Bankruptcy Act of 1978. It was a substantive change in the law that had developed over the past 50 years. The 1978 act was then amended in 1984 to add several new categories of non-dischargeable debt. In essence, the bankruptcy law had not changed much for over 100 years, from 1898 until sweeping changes enacted by Congress in 2005.[4]

The landscape of bankruptcy law in America changed dramatically on October 17, 2005. In essence, over 100 years of bankruptcy case law and history were put aside. The change in bankruptcy law essentially wiped out over 100 years of bankruptcy cases and practice and, essentially, made the filing of the Chapter 7 straight bankruptcy more

---

[3] Dixon, Timothy W., and David G. Epstein. "Where did Chapter 13 come from and where should it go?" American Bankruptcy Institute Law Review 10: 741-763.

[4] "History of Bankruptcy Law in the United States." en.wikipedia.org. http://en.wikipedia.org/wiki/History_of_bankruptcy_laws_in_the_United_States (accessed August 11, 2014).

difficult. The law attempted to push more people into filing Chapter 13 bankruptcy, which was the law originally enacted by Congress in 1938.[5]

The majority of the bankruptcy cases filed nationwide fall under consumer bankruptcies. These are types of cases filed by individual consumers under Chapter 7 straight bankruptcy and Chapter 13 debt consolidation. Of all the bankruptcies filed in our country, at least 90 percent of them fall under these two bankruptcy chapters. Let's talk a little bit about the different bankruptcy chapters now just to give the reader an overview before we discuss the substantive changes made by Congress on October 17, 2005.

Chapter 7 is commonly referred to as "straight bankruptcy." This chapter of the Bankruptcy Code essentially allows for the discharge of unsecured debts such as credit cards, medical debts, signature loans, payday advances, etc. With regard to secured debts, which are often described as items of collateral secured by a loan in which the lien holder retains an interest in the collateral, the law provides that the debtor (debtors defined as the person or entity filing the bankruptcy petition) has one of two options with regard to secured debts. He or she can either keep the item and "reaffirm" the debt and continue to pay it and re-obligate him or herself on the debt, or he or she can surrender the item to the creditor and be discharged from the debt. This can be a little tricky and it is best to discuss with your attorney whether it is advisable to "reaffirm."

There is another concept called "ride through" that should be explored with your attorney. There is also a provision under the Chapter 7 Bankruptcy Code, a "preference period," which lets creditors evaluate what was spent within a short period of time prior to the bankruptcy filing and gives several grounds for a creditor to challenge that debt as dischargeable. Again, these are issues that should be explored with your attorney.

---

5 "History of Bankruptcy." creditwrench.com. http://www.creditwrench.com/newsroom/historyofbankruptcy.html (accessed February 6, 2007).

With regard to tax debt, it is difficult to discharge tax debt, but it can be done. In simple terms, the tax debt must be older than three years before the date the bankruptcy petition was filed, all of the tax returns must have been timely filed, there can have been no offer in compromise in this intervening period, and there cannot have been an assessment by the taxing authority within 240 days of the bankruptcy filing. Again, this is a complicated area that should be explored with an attorney.

Another topic that comes up frequently is student loan debt. There used to be a provision in the Bankruptcy Code that allowed student loan debt to be discharged if the student loans were older than seven years, but that provision was rescinded by Congress in 1998. Now, the only way a student loan, both private and government guaranteed, can possibly be discharged in bankruptcy is if the debtor claims an "undue hardship." This is a very difficult standard to meet, and the case law is very much against the debtor trying to attempt an undue hardship. This should be discussed with an experienced bankruptcy attorney as it is the rare occasion that student loan debt is dischargeable.

Chapter 13 is the law that was formulated in 1938 by Congress. This law is also referred to as debtor's court, debt reorganization, or debt consolidation. In its simplest form, it is a three- to five-year payback plan of a debtor's debts. With this plan, again in its simplest form for explanation purposes, the debtor is allowed to set up a repayment plan that can catch up their mortgage and stop a foreclosure on a home. It can also stop the repossession of an automobile and pay for the balance of a vehicle through the Chapter 13 plan. It can also pay back taxes and some student loan debts. It can also serve as a vehicle to catch up child-support arrearage and pay for debts that are cosigned with another person.

Keeping in mind that approximately 90 percent of all bankruptcies fall under Chapter 7 or Chapter 13, this is probably a good time to take a moment to visit the other chapters of bankruptcy. Briefly, they are as follows:

Chapter 9 is municipal bankruptcy. It is the federal mechanism to allow for the resolution of municipal debts by cities, counties, or any type of municipality.

Chapter 11 is commonly referred to as business bankruptcy and allows for the debt reorganization of a business through bankruptcy or by an individual with substantial debts and assets. This business or corporate bankruptcy allows a company or individual to reorganize and to continue to function and remain in business while they follow the debt repayment plan laid out in the Chapter 11.

Chapter 12 is referred to as farmer bankruptcy. It allows for debt reorganization for family farmers and fishermen. Since farmers and fishermen receive their income on an irregular basis, this chapter of the Bankruptcy Code allows for that inconsistency and helps farmers and fishermen to continue to stay in business.

Let's get back to some more substantive changes made in the law under BAPCPA (Bankruptcy Abuse Prevention and Consumer Protection Act) in 2005. The biggest change that resulted from this act is the eligibility requirement based on applicable median income used for determining which chapter of bankruptcy a person may file. The change in the law also requires that debtors undergo credit counseling prior to a bankruptcy filing. The credit counseling provider must be approved by the bankruptcy court system in order for it to be accepted. Additionally, debtors must complete a financial management course during the bankruptcy in order to receive their bankruptcy discharge.

There is also a means test that is required to be completed and filed in every bankruptcy case. This is the mechanism designed in the law to force more people into filing Chapter 13 bankruptcy. If a debtor's income is deemed to be too much compared to other same-sized families in their state, then the filing of a Chapter 7 straight bankruptcy may be precluded. What the means test does is compare current monthly income (CMI) to the median family income for that family size in the particular state where that family unit resides. If it is determined the CMI is above the median income, then, as a general rule, Chapter 7 is not available. One exception to this is if the debts incurred by the debtor were primarily for business purposes. In that case, a Chapter 7 may be allowed even if the debtor is over the median income. If the debtor is above the median family income, then he or she will be required to file a Chapter 13 bankruptcy and will not be eligible for a Chapter 7. Of course, another option is for debtors to not file at all.

Statistics on bankruptcy filings have been published for the past several decades by the government. There have been a number of years where the numbers of bankruptcy filings have exceeded one million bankruptcy cases in the United States. As stated previously, it is our experience that no one comes to our offices gleefully, happy to have to be considering their problematic debt situation or the possibility of a bankruptcy filing. We tell our clients that they are not alone. In many respects, a bankruptcy filing allows a debtor or a business to start fresh and to get back into the economic swing of things. That is the reason why our founding fathers allowed for bankruptcy in the Constitution in the first place. In our capitalistic economic system, giving someone a fresh start allows them to get back into the regular flow of the economy since an individual or business laden with debt is not in a position to spend and, furthermore, cannot borrow any more money. Since bankruptcy goes back such a long way in our country's history, here is a list of just some of the famous entities and individuals that have filed for bankruptcy over the years.[6], [7]

Willie Aames – filed 2008
Abercrombie and Fitch – filed 1976

---

[6] "Famous Bankruptcies - Celebrity Research Lists." Famous Bankruptcies - Celebrity Research Lists. http://www.angelfire.com/stars4/lists/bankruptcies.html (accessed July 29, 2014).

[7] Masters, Scott. *Bankruptcy...You're Not Alone!: Famous Members of "The 7-11 Club."*: Winston-Fox, Ltd., 1997.

The Aladdin-Las Vegas – filed 1984
America West Airlines – filed 1991
Avanti Motor Corporation – filed 1985
Stephen Baldwin – filed 2009
Barneys, Inc. – filed 1996
Kim Basinger – filed 1993
Drake Bell – filed 2014
Peter Bogdanovich – filed 1985
Lorraine Bracco – filed 1999
Matthew Brady – filed 1872
Braniff Airlines – filed 1982
Toni Braxton – filed 1998 and 2010
Bridgeport, Connecticut – filed 1991
Luther Campbell of 2 Live Crew – filed 1995
Capri Beachwear, Inc. – filed 1984
Aaron Carter – filed 2013
Chelsea, Massachusetts – filed 1991
Circle K Corporation – filed 1990
Samuel Clemens a.k.a. Mark Twain – filed 1894
Coleco, Inc. – filed 1988
Gary Coleman – filed in 1999
Concrete Blonde – filed 1999
John Connally, former governor of Texas – filed 1987
Continental Airlines – filed 1983
Dr. Denton Cooley – filed 1988
Francis Ford Coppola – filed 1983, 1990, and 1992
Crazy Eddie Inc. – East Coast consumer electronics retail chain – filed 1989
DeLorean Motorcar Company – filed 1982
Delta Airlines Inc. – filed 2005
Detroit, Michigan – filed 2013
Janice Dickinson – filed 2013
Walt Disney – filed 1923
Dow Corning Corp. – filed 1995

William C. Durant – filed 1936
Lenny Dykstra – filed 2009
Eastman Kodak – filed 2012
El Paso Electric – filed 1992
Enron – filed 2001
FAO Schwartz Toy Stores – filed 2003
Federated Department Stores, Inc. – filed 1990
Financial News Network – filed 1991
Foster Grant Corporation – filed 1990
Redd Foxx – filed 1983
Frederick's of Hollywood – filed 2000
General Motors – filed 2009
Generra Sportswear Company – filed 1992
J. Ronald Getty – filed 1992
Teresa Guidice – filed 2009
Bob Guccione – filed 2003
Merle Haggard – filed 1993
Corey Haim – filed 1997
Dorothy Hamill – filed 1996
Isaac Hayes – filed 1976
Sherman Hemsley – filed 2002
Gitano Group, Inc. – filed 1994
Greyhound Lines, Inc. – filed 1990
M.C. Hammer – filed 1996
G. Heileman Brewing Company (makers of Old Style beer) – filed 1991
Milton Hershey – filed 1882
Holiday Inn – San Francisco Airport – filed 1992
Hollywood Roosevelt Hotel – filed 1989
Hyatt Regency West, Houston, Texas – filed 1986
The Improv – filed 1992
International Resort Services – filed 1993
Latoya Jackson – filed 1995
Jefferson County, Alabama – filed 2011

Chaka Khan – filed 1997
Larry King – filed 1978
K-Tel International, Inc. – filed 1984
Learjet, Inc. – filed 1990
Jerry Lee Lewis – filed 1988
Lily Rubin – filed 1996
Lionel Corporation – filed 1982
McGregor Sporting Goods – filed 1987
William McKinley – filed 1893
Marvel Entertainment Group – filed 1996
Meister Brau, Inc. – filed 1972
Midway Airlines – filed 1991
Abby Lee Miller – filed 2010
Montgomery Ward and Company – filed 1997
Myerson and Kuhn – filed 1989
Nautilus Sports/Medical Industries Inc. – filed 1990
New York Daily News – filed 1991
Wayne Newton Gaming Inc. and Wayne Newton individually – filed 1992
Nutrisystem, Inc. – filed 1993
Ocean Pacific Sunwear, LTD – filed 1992
Orange County, California – filed 1994
Orion Pictures Corporation – filed 1991
Pan American World Airways – filed 1991
Pantera's Corporation – file 1989
Paramount Studios – filed 1932
Peaches Records and Tapes – filed 1981
Penn Central Transportation Company – filed 1970
Pepsi Cola Company – filed 1923
Tom Petty – filed 1979
Pic and Save – filed 1995
Planet Hollywood International, Inc. – filed 1999 and 2001
Polaroid Corporation – filed 2001
Susan Powter – filed 1995

PTL – filed 1987
Purina Mills – filed 1999
Reader's Digest Assn. – filed 2009
Regal Cinemas – filed 2001
Rembrandt – filed 1656
Resorts International – filed 1989
Revco DS, Inc. – filed 1988
Burt Reynolds – filed 1996
Debbie Reynolds – filed 1987
Ronco Products, Inc. – filed 1984
Mickey Rooney – filed 1962
Saab Automobile – filed 2011
San Jose California United School District – filed 1983
Sbarro, Inc. – filed 2011
Schwinn Bicycle Company – filed 1992
Six Flags, Inc. – filed 2009
Sizzler International Inc. – filed 1996
Smith-Corona Corp. – filed 1995
Anna Nicole Smith – filed 1996
South Tucson, Arizona – filed 1983
Lynn Spears – filed 1998
Stan Lee Media – filed 2001
Standard Brands Paint Company – filed 1992
StarCraft Corporation – filed 1990
Studio 54 – filed 1985
Sunbeam Corp. – filed 2001
Sun-Times Media Group, Inc. – filed 2009
Lawrence Taylor – filed 2009
Telemundo Group, Inc. – filed 1993
Texaco, Inc. – filed 1987
Trans World Airlines – filed 1992
Tribune Group – filed 2008
Mike Tyson – filed 2003
Johnny Unitas – filed 1991

United Press International – filed 1985
US Airways – filed 2002
Michael Vick – filed 2008
Vision Craft – filed 1990
Vlasic Foods International, Inc. – filed 2001
Dionne Warwick – filed 2013
Western Union Corp. – filed 1993
Wheeling-Pittsburgh Steel Corporation – filed 1985
Oscar Wilde – filed 1895
Winn Dixie Stores, Inc. – filed 2005
Yellow Cab Company – filed 1976
Zale Corporation – filed 1999
Zenith Electronics Corporation – filed 1999

This is by no means an exhaustive, complete list. Plenty of famous and well-known people and companies have filed for bankruptcy. Many of the most prominent and famous members in each community throughout our country have had to file for bankruptcy at some point in their history. This list is not meant to point at any specific individual or company out there but just to let people know that bad things, to include financial problems, can happen to everybody. There is relief, and our Constitution allows for individuals and companies to restart their lives. There is a way to start fresh, and bankruptcy specifically provides that fresh start. Many of the names on this list have recovered and are important and instrumental people and entities in our society. Look at it this way—if bankruptcy was not available, then probably one of the most famous people on this list, Walt Disney, would not have the impact on the millions of us that he has had and will continue to have over the years to come.

The government publishes bankruptcy statistics each year that cover all bankruptcy filings nationwide. As you can see, the majority of filings are consumer bankruptcies.

Annual Business and Non-business Filings by Year (1980–2013)[8]

Year	Total Filings	Business Filings	Non-Business Filings	Consumer Filings as a Percentage of Total Filings
1980	331,264	43,694	287,570	86.81%
1981	363,943	48,125	315,818	86.78%
1982	380,251	69,300	310,951	81.78%
1983	348,880	62,436	286,444	82.10%
1984	348,521	64,004	284,517	81.64%
1985	412,510	71,277	341,233	82.72%
1986	530,438	81,235	449,203	84.69%
1987	577,999	82,446	495,553	85.74%
1988	613,465	63,853	549,612	89.59%
1989	679,461	63,235	616,226	90.69%
1990	782,960	64,853	718,107	91.72%
1991	943,987	71,549	872,438	92.42%
1992	971,517	70,643	900,874	92.73%
1993	875,202	62,304	812,898	92.88%
1994	832,829	52,374	780,455	93.71%
1995	926,601	51,959	874,642	94.39%
1996	1,178,555	53,549	1,125,006	95.46%
1997	1,404,145	54,027	1,350,118	96.15%
1998	1,442,549	44,367	1,398,182	96.92%
1999	1,319,465	37,884	1,281,581	97.12%
2000	1,253,444	35,472	1,217,972	97.17%

[8] "Annual Business and Non-business Filings by Year (1980-2012)." American Bankruptcy Institute. http://www.abiworld.org/AM/AMTemplate.cfm?Section=Home&TEMPLATE=/CM/ContentDisplay.cfm&CONTENTID=66471 (accessed August 11, 2014).

2001	1,492,129	40,099	1,452,030	97.31%
2002	1,577,651	38,540	1,539,111	97.56%
2003	1,660,245	35,037	1,625,208	97.89%
2004	1,597,462	34,317	1,563,145	97.85%
2005	2,078,415	39,201	2,039,214	98.11%
2006	617,660	19,695	597,965	96.81%
2007	850,912	28,322	822,590	96.67%
2008	1,117,771	43,456	1,074,225	96.10%
2009	1,473,675	60,837	1,412,838	95.87%
2010	1,593,081	56,282	1,536,799	96.47%
2011	1,410,653	47,806	1,362,874	96.61%
2012	1,221,091	40,075	1,181,016	96.72%
2013[1]	1,071,932	33,212	1,038,720	96.90%

1 "Table F-2. U.S. Bankruptcy Courts – Business and Non-business Cases Commenced, by Chapter of the Bankruptcy Code, During the 12-Month Period Ending December 31, 2013." United States Courts. http://www.uscourts.gov/uscourts/Statistics/BankruptcyStatistics/BankruptcyFilings/2013/1213_f2.pdf (accessed August 11, 2014)..

Chapter 5

Moral Guidance and Thoughts on Debt

By now, you should have picked up from this book the fact that no one files for bankruptcy lightly. It is a tough, stressful, and worry-laden decision. By the time people come to see us, they have already had a great deal of stress, worry, sleepless nights, and consternation over their debts, not to mention the collection calls, letters, lawsuits, foreclosure letters, etc. We always approach every client with the mind-set that each person wants to pay their debts, if at all possible. Quite frankly, this is a good situation for a prospective client of ours to actually file a Chapter 13 bankruptcy plan, which would allow that person to pay their debts either in full or in part, whatever they can do, while still being able to provide for themselves and their families. From a moral perspective, everyone has to wrestle and deal with their own views individually. In this light, attorney O. Max Gardner, a nationally known and highly regarded consumer bankruptcy expert from North Carolina, has written an illustrative article on bankruptcy and the Bible. It may be of some benefit to the reader here.

Forgive Us Our Debts as We Forgive Our Debtors
Bankruptcy and the Bible
By Attorney O. Max Gardner, Shelbyville, North Carolina
Reprinted with permission

Dalton Camp proclaimed several years ago that, "having lost its value, money may no longer be the root of all evil; credit having taken its place." This statement demonstrates the paradox of modern day religion and debt—should our reaction be one of condemnation or one of compassion. Since many recent respected studies have shown that the average American family is only three weeks away from personal bankruptcy, and new legislation that will deny bankruptcy relief to hundreds of thousands of American families is now the law, it is time to revisit what the Bible teaches us about debt.

The Bible makes it clear that people are generally expected to pay their debts. Leviticus 25:39. No one will—or should—advance any argument against this general proposition. However, this moral and legal obligation to pay just debts must be balanced by such considerations as the need for compassion and the call to cancel debts at periodic intervals. The Biblical basis for such considerations is based on the Sabbatical and Jubilee years. The secular basis arises out of the Constitutional requirement that Congress enact uniform laws allowing businesses and consumers to cancel and to restructure debt obligations. This Biblical support for the legal right to cancel debt is enforced by the even stronger Biblical doctrine that prohibited interest *of any amount* rather than just usury or excessive interest.

Within the areas of economic justice and stability, the Old Testament is replete with examples of compassionate treatment of the poor, and with preservation of the family unit. These goals were superior to the material concerns of repayment of debt. For instance, Deuteronomy 15:7-10 is particularly forceful. It provides as follows: "If there is a poor man among your brothers…do not be hardhearted or tightfisted toward your poor brother. Rather be open-handed and freely lend him whatever he needs. Be careful not to harbor this wicked thought: 'The seventh year, the year for canceling debts, is near,' so that you show ill toward your needy brother and give him nothing. He may then appeal to the LORD against you, and you will be found guilty of sin. Give generously to him and do so without a grudging heart; then because of this the LORD your God will bless you in all your work and in everything you put your hands to."

The cancellation of debt in the Old Testament was accomplished at legislated intervals. Deuteronomy 15:1-2 clearly provides for such legislative release with the following language: "At the end of every seven years you shall grant a release. And this is the manner of the release: every creditor shall release what he has lent to his neighbor, his brother, because the Lord's release has been proclaimed." Under this Biblical model, the debtors' payment or non-payment of debts was not in question. The debtors may or may not have been culpable for their debts. It was a strict model with no "means test" or detailed analysis of every debt.[9] And, while Old Testament lenders were admonished to be merciful, debts were canceled every seven years whether they liked it or not. The Old Testament model can therefore be legitimately applied to modern day bankruptcy laws. The principle is that, while taken seriously, debt can be canceled to achieve some higher purpose—such as the preservation of the family unit. It also should be noted that Deuteronomy 15:12-13 provides that slaves should be freed every seven years, creating an interesting analogy between the creditor-debtor and the master-servant relationship.

The Biblical use of the term "usury" corresponds to our modern word "interest" rather than to the notion of "excessive interest" to which we generally apply the term usury today. Only a small number of us would seriously question the morality of profiting from a loan at normal interest rates. However, the Talmud quotes an ancient rabbi as saying: "It is better to sell your daughter into slavery than to borrow money on interest." The Lord only knows what this same rabbi would say today if confronted with credit cards bearing interest rates of 34.99% and higher and with some "pay day" lenders demanding annual rates in excess of 2,000%.

---

[9] This passage is similar to many other Old Testament commandments, including Deuteronomy 5:17's "Thou shall not kill," which provides no specifics nor creates no hierarchy of culpability.

The Biblical doctrine of usury rests primarily on three texts: Exodus 22:25; Leviticus 25:35; and Deuteronomy 23:19-20. Exodus and Leviticus prohibit loans of money or food with interest to a needy brother or sister or even a resident alien. Deuteronomy forbids taking interest from any person. Other Books of the Bible underline the importance of this prohibition on interest. For example, Psalm 15:5 characterizes a righteous man as one who, among other things, "lends his money without usury." Both Ezekiel 22:12 and Nehemiah 5:0-11 condemn lending money with interest, especially to the poor. And Ezekiel 18:13 lists the taking of interest among sins worthy of death.

The prohibition on interest is based on God's covenant with Israel. The rule is founded upon the compassionate treatment of various oppressed groups: the resident alien; the widow; the orphans; and the poor. Exodus 22:25-27 states the law in explicit terms: "If you lend to one of my people among you who is needy, do not be like the money lender; charge him no interest. If you take your neighbor's cloak as a pledge, return it to him by sunset, because his cloak is the only covering he has for his body. What else will he sleep on? When he cries out to me, I will hear, for I am compassionate." Leviticus 25:35-37 provides that "If one of your countrymen becomes poor and is unable to support himself among you, help him as you would an alien or a temporary resident, so that he can continue to live among you. Do not take interest of any kind from him, but fear your God, so that your countryman may continue to live among you. You must not lend him money at interest or sell him food at profit." Finally, Deuteronomy 23:19-20 provides: "Do not charge your brother interest, whether on money or food or anything else that may earn interest."

Jesus clearly had these Biblical principles in mind when he admonished the "money changers" and removed them from God's house, the sacred Temple. In John 2:14 Jesus "poured out the changers of money and overthrew the tables." Jesus, in fact, was always true to the principles underlying usury and debt forgiveness and the notion of the importance of placing love and compassion above greed and wealth. In Luke 6:34-35 Jesus said: "And if you lend to those from whom you hope to receive, what credit is that to you? Even sinners lend to sinners, to receive as much again. But love your enemies and, do good, and lend, expecting nothing in return, and your reward will be great, and you will be sons of the Most High; for he is kind to the ungrateful and the selfish." The followers of Jesus were to be concerned with the welfare of others, even when met with hatred and abuse.

The consistent teaching of both the Old and New Testaments is that compassion, mercy, and justice are to override purely economic concerns, such as loans. Religious people are to be gracious to all, even debtors. Jesus said that God does cause the rain to fall on the just and the unjust and in Mark 10:25 he said that "[i]t is easier for a camel to go through the eye of a needle, than for a rich man to enter in to the kingdom of God." And in Luke 16:9 he said: "I tell you, use worldly wealth to gain friends for yourselves, so that when it is gone, you will be welcomed into eternal dwellings," and to "forgive and ye shall be forgiven" Luke 6:37.

The compassion of the scriptures, including the setting aside of legitimate rights of lenders, was typical of economic relationships in the economy of early Judeo-Christian societies. The central theme is one of stability—a stable society with a guarantee of economic security to each family. Wealth was viewed as a blessing from God (Deuteronomy 8:11-18, 28). This blessing resulted from obedience and was based on God's compassion. The tithing for the poor, the gleaning laws, the year of the Jubilee, were all tangible ways that Israelites could show compassion for each other and honor God by following His law. Beyond income-maintenance programs, the Biblical Law provided a permanent mechanism—such as the Sabbatical year and Jubilee—to ensure that temporary misfortune barred no family from full participation in economic life.

The current bankruptcy law passed by Congress and signed into law by the President in 2005 lacks any compassion for the poor, makes no redress to the modern day money changers who shamelessly peddle plastic at rates that would draw the Holy wrath of God himself, provides no relief but only additional misery to the families saddled with thousands of dollars in medical bills, and most importantly severely undermines the economic and social stability of the average American family. These Americans are like the farmers of the Old Testament who proclaimed to King Nehemiah, "We have had to borrow money to pay the king's tax on our fields and vineyards. Although we are of the same flesh and blood as our countrymen and though our sons are as good as theirs, yet we have to subject our sons and daughters to slavery. Some of our daughters have already been enslaved, but we are powerless, because our fields and our vineyards belong to others" Nehemiah 5:3-5. Nehemiah responded to his people and ordered to "let the extracting of usury stop! Give back to them immediately their fields, vineyards, olive groves, and houses and also the usury you are charging them…" Nehemiah 5:11. It is time for our elected Representatives in Washington to follow the example of the Holy Scriptures and to respond in kind by repealing the current Bankruptcy Bill and by not taking away power from the powerless and eliminating relief for the suffering.

Based on an article by O. Max Gardner, III, Esquire (maxgardner@maxgardner.com)

Chapter 6

Getting Started With Us (How to Get Your Credit Reports)

As discussed previously, someone with financial questions or issues comes to us and meets with one of our licensed attorneys for a free consultation. At this consultation, potential clients are most likely concerned about their debt situation, and they have already either received collection calls and the like or are concerned about how their immediate credit future looks. Our prospective clients will fill out an information form that we can provide to them at our office or we can email to them or direct them to our website to fill it out. Either way, what we suggest before the prospective client starts with us is for them to get control of their situation. As the saying goes, knowledge is power. We recommend that clients write out every single bill that they have, starting with all of their current monthly bills as far as rent or mortgage payments, utilities, food costs, insurance costs, and the like. Once that is done, we ask our prospective clients to gather together all of the bills that they have to include home loans, car loans, medical debts, credit card debt, signature loans, payday advances, and any other type of debt. Immediately after doing that, to make sure this exercise is full and complete, the next thing all of our prospective clients should do is to get their credit reports. Nationwide, there are three main credit reporting agencies that provide virtually all of the credit information in the United States. These credit reporting agencies are Experian, Equifax, and TransUnion. I recently wrote an article for the BondandBotes.com blog on this issue and am including it below for the reader's convenience.

HOW CAN I GET MY FREE CREDIT REPORTS?
By Attorney Ronald C. Sykstus

Pursuant to the Federal Trade Commission (FTC) rules, all individuals in the United States are entitled to one free credit report each 12 months from each of the three credit reporting agencies: Equifax, Experian, and TransUnion. The **ONLY WAY** to get your actual, true free credit reports is from **www.annualcreditreport.com. You can also call the toll-free number and request them over the phone. 877-322-8228**

If you are contemplating a bankruptcy filing, it is, in our opinion, acceptable to get your credit reports directly from the website, **www.annualcreditreport.com. Before** you go to this website, PLEASE make sure your computer is attached to a **working printer** and that you **PRINT** all pages of **ALL** of your credit reports as you will only be able to view them one time and you will NOT be able to visit the site again. **This is very important!**

If, however, you need credit reports for any other purpose and, most importantly, if you are contesting something you think should not be on your credit reports, **DO NOT** get the credit reports online at this site. What you need to do is to get the mail-in form from **www.annualcreditreport.com** and fill it out and physically mail it in to the Atlanta address on the form itself. For credit report **disputes and errors**, it is very important that you do not agree to any type of binding arbitration which may preclude you from filing a lawsuit if your credit reports are damaged through no fault of your own. As a result, it is advisable to get your credit reports this way only if you believe you will have to dispute your credit report. **As a general rule and as explained above, for bankruptcy purposes, getting all three credit reports online, again, is acceptable and it is probably the quickest way for you to get them**. Please note that sometimes when you mail in the form for the request, you may be told by that website that it cannot verify that you are who you say you are. As a result, when you mail the form in, you may want to include a utility bill or a phone bill or some type of bill that ties you to the address where you state that you reside, which is where the credit reports will be mailed.

If you are contemplating a bankruptcy filing and you want to get your credit reports for that purpose and you are having difficulty getting your free credit reports from www.annualcreditreports.com then, given the **warning above**, you can get your credit reports by paying for them directly from the credit reporting agencies online at their websites:

www.experian.com
Experian
701 Experian Parkway
Allen, TX 75013

www.equifax.com
Equifax
1550 Peachtree Street NW
Atlanta, GA 30309-2468

www.transunion.com
TransUnion
555 West Adams Street
Chicago, IL 60661

Finally, you can also mail the credit reporting agencies to get your credit reports. When requesting your personal credit report in writing directly from the credit reporting agencies, using personal check or money order, you must provide the following information with your request:

1. First, middle, and last name (including Jr., Sr., III)
2. Your current address
3. Previous addresses in the past five years, if any

4. Your social security number
5. Your date of birth, current employer, phone number, signature
6. Applicable fee ($12.95)

Expect a 14-business-day waiting period to receive your copy in the mail.

One final word of caution here: If, while reading this chapter, you realize that your only issue is that you want to dispute errors or mistakes on your credit report, then do not do anything until you've read and familiarized yourself with the Fair Credit Reporting Act (FCRA). There is a separate chapter later on in this book about the Fair Credit Reporting Act.

Chapter 7

Effect of Bankruptcy on a Credit Report and How to Improve a Credit Report After a Bankruptcy Filing

This is a common concern of almost all of the clients who come to our office. My partner, Brad Botes, wrote the article below for the BondandBotes.com blog that explains the effect bankruptcy has on a credit report.

How Will Bankruptcy Affect My Credit?
By Attorney Bradford W. Botes

Virtually every person who comes to see us to talk about a potential bankruptcy filing asks us this question in one form or another. They may have been told by a friend that bankruptcy will ruin their credit. Another has heard that they won't be able to get new credit for seven to ten years. In short, most folks want to know how a bankruptcy filing will affect their credit.

The truth is that, by the time an individual makes it into our office to discuss bankruptcy, their credit is usually already in bad shape. They may have gotten behind on mortgage or car payments. Perhaps a foreclosure or repossession has already occurred. Some people have managed to keep their credit score high, but they are simply borrowing from one creditor to make minimum payments to another. We call this robbing Peter to pay Paul. The credit score may be okay but the last thing they can do, or want to do, is to borrow more money. The point is that bankruptcy doesn't ruin your credit; it is what has taken place prior to filing bankruptcy that does so.

The great majority of our clients are honest people. The credit problems that they have had are often through no fault of their own. It may have been a job loss, an illness, or even a divorce; but for whatever reason, they are unable to pay their bills as they become due. Often, bankruptcy can be the first step in helping to turn around their credit worthiness.

But how can this be? How can bankruptcy make a person's credit better? Step back and think about that question from an objective perspective. Say a lady who has never filed bankruptcy goes to a bank to borrow money. She has thousands of dollars in credit card debt. She is behind on her car payment. The truth is that she can't pay the bills that she has now, let alone the payments on the new loan that she is asking the banker to give her. Plus, if the banker were to give her the loan, she could file bankruptcy on all of her creditors, including the banker, shortly thereafter.

Now say this same lady makes the tough decision to file a Chapter 7 bankruptcy and she receives a discharge of all of her credit card debt. She surrenders her car with payments that were too high and discharges the balance owed. A year later, she goes to the same banker to borrow money to buy a less expensive car with lower payments. She is honest and tells the banker that she filed bankruptcy a year earlier. He considers this but also considers the fact that she now no longer has any credit card debt or a high car payment. Perhaps most importantly, she can't file another Chapter 7 bankruptcy until eight years after the prior case was filed. So if he makes the loan, it will be the only debt that she will have to pay and she cannot discharge the debt in bankruptcy. Objectively, she is a much better loan risk now than she was a year earlier. Of course, all of this assumes that she acts responsibly after her bankruptcy discharge.

The point here is that, if your credit is already in bad shape or overextended and the stress of dealing with the situation is becoming overwhelming, it may be time to sit down with a bankruptcy attorney and at least learn your options. As we have said often, don't be fooled by someone you don't know at the other end of an 800 number. Our firm offers a free consultation during which you will meet with an experienced bankruptcy attorney. We won't just pass you off to a secretary or paralegal. One of our attorneys will meet with you face-to-face and help you explore your options. Don't let what you have heard about how bankruptcy may affect your credit keep you from doing this. The real question is—what condition will your credit be in a year from now if you don't do something?

The following discussion covers what a person can do to improve credit after a bankruptcy filing.

How Can I Improve My Credit After Filing for Bankruptcy?
By Attorney Ronald C. Sykstus

This is a question that we often get asked when someone is contemplating filing for bankruptcy. First of all, if someone has perfect credit, meaning that they have never been behind on any debts, then filing for bankruptcy will hurt their credit dramatically. If, however, someone is already behind on their debts and they are receiving collection calls, collection letters, and threats of lawsuit, then, in all likelihood, the credit is already bad and hurt, and filing for bankruptcy will not make it worse.

A bankruptcy filing can stay a person's credit for period of ten years from the date of filing, regardless whether Chapter 7 or Chapter 13 bankruptcy was filed. This is compared to "bad" credit, which are the late payments and the like, and they can remain on the credit report for a period of seven years from the date of last activity, which is either when the debt has been paid in full or the creditor has charged off the debt, which is an internal accounting mechanism. Please note that a "charge off" does not mean that the debt has gone away—it will most likely simply be sold or assigned to another debt collector.

Our initial advice to our clients' concerns in ensuring that their credit will improve after a bankruptcy filing is to make sure that all of their debts are listed in the bankruptcy petition. This includes any conceivable debt or bill that a person may owe along with any debt collector or collection agency that is trying to collect on the debt itself. Once the debts are listed, the next goal is to obtain a discharge in bankruptcy. That is the end goal of a bankruptcy case. Once that is done, get your free credit reports in writing only from www.annualcreditreport.com. I have already explained why, especially at this juncture, they should be obtained in writing only!

Once you receive your credit reports, all that can be listed for each discharged debt is that the debt has been "discharged in bankruptcy" and it has to reflect a zero (0) balance. It cannot reflect that it is past due, charged off, in collections, or that any type of balance is due and owing. If each debt that you discharged in bankruptcy is not reflected this way, there is a specific and certain way to put these items in dispute with the credit reporting agencies. The dispute process under the Fair Credit Reporting Act (FCRA) requires that any erroneous information on a credit report must be disputed with the credit reporting agency itself (Equifax, Experian, TransUnion) and NOT the furnisher of the incorrect information. This is the only way to trigger liability to ensure it gets corrected. The dispute letter should be signed and dated and mailed by certified mail, return receipt. Keep a copy of the letter that is mailed and the returned green card to ensure they got it. Do not do this dispute any other way! When you prepare your written dispute, you will state, "I am disputing this erroneous credit information noted because (name of creditor/collector) is listed in collections (or however it is listed) and with a balance of $X. I have attached a copy of my bankruptcy discharge and the pertinent schedules showing that this creditor was discharged in bankruptcy. As a result, all that should be listed on this debt is zero balance and discharged in bankruptcy. Please correct this information and, pursuant to the Fair Credit Reporting Act, please forward this information to the credit furnisher." Make sure the letter is dated and signed and keep a copy of it before you mail it by certified mail, return receipt requested.

Finally, once you ensure that all of the debts you discharged in bankruptcy are reflected on your credit reports as a zero (0) balance and "included in bankruptcy," make sure you stay absolutely current on your regular and current monthly bills, which will enhance your "good" credit. Most people recover quite nicely after a discharge and are able to move on in a positive fashion with their lives, including getting back the ability to obtain credit on reasonable terms.

Chapter 8

Should I Use a Debt Management Company or a Debt Relief Company to Handle My Debts?

Our unqualified and immediate answer to this question is no! Since this is such a widely discussed topic and one that sounds so wonderful on the radio, TV, and Internet, our attorneys address this question daily. You might logically think that we have a vested interest in telling prospective clients not to use these types of debt settlement companies since we practice in the area of consumer bankruptcy law, but I assure you that is not the case at all. Our answer is based upon hundreds and hundreds of clients who have been cheated out of their money, credit, and time by using these types of companies and going through this process, which universally fails, before coming to see us. Three of our attorneys, Brad Botes, Carla Handy, and Ed Woods express their views on this topic here.

Should I Use a Debt Settlement Company?
By Attorney Bradford W. Botes

The ads on the radio always sound alluring. Simply respond by calling a toll-free number and the debt settlement company will solve all of your financial problems. But is the promised relief as good as described?

Debt Settlement Process

The business model, or pitch, works something like this. You will be instructed to stop paying on your credit cards and to instead make payments to the debt settlement company. Often, the company will want to deduct the money straight from your bank account. You are told that the credit card companies will eventually give up and write the debt off. They will then sell your debt to some third-party debt buyer for pennies on the dollar. By that time, the debt settlement company will have amassed enough of your money to settle the claims of the credit card companies. They will pay everything off and your credit will be perfect. The radio ad says that you will be able to buy a new house and/or car in very little time.

There are a number of problems with this business model. First and foremost is that you are sending your hard-earned money to a company you know little about. In many cases, you are even providing your bank account information. The debt settlement industry is largely unregulated. A simple Internet search will reveal that there are volumes of people who have sent money to these companies and not obtained any relief at all. By the time they realize that the plan is not working as described, the company that they sent their money to is nowhere to be found. The money is not traceable.

In addition to the above, even if the plan works as described, the individual's credit report will still show numerous late payments and/or write-offs. These are not going to help the individual's credit score. Potentially even more costly is the fact that new tax liability may be created. When a creditor forgives debt, the amount forgiven can be treated as income by the Internal Revenue Service. Taxes may become due on that income.

If you are a consumer struggling with debt, your best option may be to meet face-to-face with a qualified and experienced consumer bankruptcy attorney. The attorney will have passed a bar exam, he will be licensed by a state bar association, and his work will be scrutinized by a judge. A good bankruptcy attorney will help you to explore all of your options—both bankruptcy and non-bankruptcy.

The fact is that you owe it to yourself to fully explore all of your options. Financial problems can be stressful for you and your family. Don't necessarily take what sounds like the easiest solution. In many cases, decisions like this will have contributed to the financial problems that you now face.

Is a Debt Settlement Program Better Than Filing for Bankruptcy?
By Attorney Carla M. Handy

Most likely you have some familiarity with companies offering debt settlement programs as an alternative to filing for bankruptcy. You may have seen commercials on television offering to reduce your debt 50 percent or more and offering a plan to get you out of debt within a short period of time. It almost seems too good to be true and, generally speaking, it is. Often a person will opt for such a program because they believe it will not harm their credit as much as a bankruptcy filing. In reality, a debt settlement program can be far more detrimental to your credit score than a bankruptcy and prolong the misery of being overwhelmed by debt.

A debt settlement program generally works like this: After providing a debt settlement company with information as to who and how much you owe, the company generates a payment plan for you and instructs you to stop making payments to your creditors and begin making payments to them while they are negotiating settlements with your creditors. The debt settlement company will collect a fee from the moneys you are paying into the plan that consists of either a percentage of your monthly payment or a percentage of the settlement deal they reach with each of your creditors. It sounds great but the devil is in the details, and a lot of these companies will not fully inform you of how the system really works. First, by instructing you to stop paying your creditors, the debt settlement company is intentionally pushing your account into charge-off status with the creditor with the hope the creditor will, at that point, then be willing to settle for a reduced amount of the debt. This charge-off status on the account will, most likely, result in a negative item on your credit report that can remain on the report for up to seven years. In addition, there is no guarantee the creditor will agree to accept a reduced settlement even after the account has reached charged-off status. Second, once you stop making payments to your creditors, you will likely experience collection calls from your creditors and, ultimately, collection lawsuits. The reason? Most debt settlement companies do not negotiate these settlements with your creditors all at one time but, instead, one by one. While one creditor is being paid you will likely be subject to collection efforts by other creditors who are receiving nothing. And these collection efforts can result in judgments that can become liens against your property or subject your wages or your bank accounts to garnishment. Finally, even when a reduced settlement is reached with a creditor, the amount of the reduction can be turned into the IRS as debt forgiveness income and subject to a tax consequence.

Bankruptcy can often be a far better option than a debt settlement program. It is a process that has a defined beginning and end with protection from collection efforts from your creditors while you are in that process. While it will also be a negative item on your credit report, your credit score can begin to improve as soon as the bankruptcy is completed.

Can You Work Out Your Debts on Your Own?
By Attorney Ed Woods

Yes, you can. There is no law that says you must seek any formal, legal debt relief. For example, you can contact your creditors at any time and inform them that you're having a hard time making ends meet and ask them to work with you. You might ask them to reduce your monthly payments. Or, perhaps they would be willing to take less than the balance owed if you pay the reduced balance in a lump sum. Be aware that if you convince a creditor to accept less than the full balance you owe, you may be creating a tax problem for yourself. But, you can take this overall approach with every single creditor you owe in an effort to get your finances under control. Some of your creditors may even be willing to help you, but they are not under any legal duty to do so. In other words, you may ask for help, but the creditor has a legal right to say no.

The Self-Help Approach

If you are in this situation, the real question is whether or not it makes any sense at all to try this self-help approach. You're going to have to talk these creditors out of some money that you legally owe. Most creditors take the position that they loaned you the money and you should pay it back as you agreed. If your financial problems are stemming from one or two creditors, then you might try to work out something with just these creditors. If you can successfully accomplish this, then you've resolved your financial crisis for the present and more formal debt relief may not be necessary.

On the other hand, if your financial troubles stem from more than just a few creditors or you have "super" creditors like the IRS, student loans, or past-due alimony or child support, you very likely need to seriously consider formal, legal debt relief.

Credit Counseling Agencies

You might be thinking about contacting a credit counseling agency. Reputable credit counseling agencies can give you advice about managing your money and debts, help you develop a budget, and offer free educational materials and workshops. Counselors in reputable credit counseling agencies are trained and certified in the areas of consumer credit, money and debt management, and budgeting. These agencies may be able to help you develop a "debt management plan" or DMP.

If you're thinking about contacting a credit counseling agency, the first thing you should consider is whether or not the services of a credit counseling agency are likely to cure your troubles. In making this determination, you should ask yourself some questions. Are you disciplined enough to create a realistic budget for yourself and stick to it? If not, credit counseling probably won't help you. Are at least some of your creditors willing or likely to work with you on repaying the debt you owe? If not, credit counseling may be ineffective. Which of your debts is causing the most problems? Credit counseling agencies can usually help only in certain situations when all you need is a little lowering of your interest rates on some unsecured debts, e.g., credit cards. If your financial problems include past-due balances on your house note, car payment, or other payment on debts secured by collateral, credit counseling agencies will rarely, if ever, be able to help you. In these situations, you are facing the real possibility that you are about to lose your home in a foreclosure or your car to a repossession. And that foreclosure or repossession is likely to come sooner rather than later, so time is of the essence. And, as mentioned above, if you owe delinquent taxes, student loans, and/or past-due alimony or child support, it is highly unlikely that you will resolve these types of debt through a credit counseling agency.

If you are being sued for the collection of a debt, a credit counseling agency cannot help you. In such situations, you need legal advice, not credit counseling assistance. Be aware that if you are being sued, you should seek the advice of a competent and experienced debt relief lawyer immediately. Once a lawsuit is filed against you, you have only a limited amount of time to formally respond to the lawsuit. If you do not respond within that time, a judgment by default can be entered against you. If this happens, you normally lose your right to contest the lawsuit even if you had good grounds to do so. In this situation, your only recourse is normally bankruptcy under Chapter 7 or debt consolidation under Chapter 13.

Further, if you are considering the services of a credit counseling agency, you should be very careful and search for a reputable agency. Some agencies call themselves "nonprofit"; however, this does not mean their services are free of charge. Some credit counseling agencies charge high fees and may not disclose all fees to you. It is probably best to locate a credit counseling agency that offers local, in-person services in your area. Many universities, military bases, credit unions, housing authorities, and branches of the U. S. Cooperative Extension

Service operate nonprofit credit counseling programs. Your financial institution, family, and friends may be good sources of information and referral.

Bankruptcy May Be the Best Solution

Although self-help may work in certain circumstances, always remember that there are no self-help remedies that will protect you and your money and property from foreclosures, repossessions, lawsuits, bank account and wage garnishments, seizure of non-exempt assets, and collection harassment. And, as mentioned above, credit counseling agencies cannot help you in these circumstances. Only formal, legal debt relief can protect you from these consequences. If you are faced with any of these possibilities, you need immediate legal advice from a competent and experienced debt relief attorney. Our attorneys have been helping families and individuals deal with these matters for decades.

Chapter 9

Do I Lose Everything I Own When I File for Bankruptcy and What Property Can I Protect?

Clients who come to our office often worry whether they will lose any or all of their property if they file for bankruptcy. It is a very rare occurrence where a person who files for bankruptcy will actually lose any of his or her property. There is a concept called exemptions, which is the specific allowance under either federal or state law that sets forth a certain amount of property of all types (personal property, clothing, tools of the trade, automobiles, retirement assets, etc.) that people are allowed to retain when they file for bankruptcy, being that the property is exempt from creditors. It may also be dependent upon which chapter of bankruptcy a person elects to file or whether that property is secured by a lien. A few of our attorneys explain these exemptions below, along with some general comments as they relate to the concept of exemption.

Will I Lose Everything I Own If I File Bankruptcy?
By Attorney Bradford W. Botes

Many people who come to see us about bankruptcy are concerned about losing their property. There is a misconception that, upon filing for bankruptcy protection from your creditors, the court will take your home, car, and furniture. The truth is that, in the vast majority of bankruptcy cases filed by individuals, absolutely no property is taken or sold by the court.

It is true that upon filing for bankruptcy, the court will appoint a trustee to review the individual's belongings and, if appropriate, to sell the assets for the benefit of the person's creditors. If the case is filed properly, however, there will be no assets to be sold by the trustee. Debtors who file bankruptcy have the right to protect, or claim as exempt, certain assets as they move beyond bankruptcy. The amount and type of property that a debtor can claim as exempt will be generally be determined by the state in which the debtor lives. Each state has either created its own exemptions or adopted certain federal exemptions. In many cases, these exemptions will allow the debtor to keep his home, automobile, and other assets. It should be noted that this does not mean that the property will be owned free and clear. If the debtor owes money against her property, such as a mortgage or car loan, she will be required to keep paying that loan following the bankruptcy in order to keep the property. This is often done through what bankruptcy attorneys call a reaffirmation agreement. It is a commitment to keep paying for the collateral after the bankruptcy filing.

In some circumstances, the person filing bankruptcy will own more property than he can protect, or claim as exempt, in the bankruptcy case. Even in this situation, however, he will be able to maintain the property by filing a Chapter 13 bankruptcy. In this type of bankruptcy, the debtor will work with his attorney to formulate a plan to pay the creditors over a three- to five-year period the amount that the creditors would have received if his assets had been liquidated. Chapter 13 for an individual is similar to what large corporations often do through a Chapter 11 bankruptcy. The debtor keeps the assets he needs to effectively reorganize his finances while being protected by the bankruptcy court.

Brad then contrasts exempt property being protected above as compared to property that has a lien against it. The question is whether you can keep secured property in bankruptcy.

Can You File Bankruptcy and Keep Your House and Car?
By Attorney Bradford W. Botes

As an attorney who has been helping people obtain bankruptcy protection for over 25 years, I am still amazed at some of the misconceptions people have about bankruptcy. Whether at my kid's school, at church, or elsewhere in the community, someone will tell me about a "friend," "acquaintance," or "coworker" who filed bankruptcy and kept their house, car, and valuable possessions. They are often under the impression that the individual kept all of these items and didn't pay for them. This is simply not the case. If the house, car, or other property has a valid lien against it, the lien will usually survive the bankruptcy. In other words, if the property is to be kept, it usually must be paid for. The important point here is that people who seek bankruptcy protection can often afford their current house and car payment once they rid themselves of credit card, medical, and other unsecured debt. The bankruptcy process can help an honest individual keep a roof over her head and transportation to and from work by getting rid of other debt.

Even better yet, the bankruptcy process can help someone who is behind on house or car payments catch up what they are behind and stop a repossession or foreclosure. Chapter 13 of the Bankruptcy Code allows an individual to stop a foreclosure or repossession and propose a plan to pay the amount behind over a period of up to 60 months. This can be done while paying only a small percentage, if anything, toward credit card and/or medical bills. Taxes, student loans, and even back child support can be provided for in the plan of reorganization.

The point here is that you should not give up if you are behind on house or car payments. A competent and experienced consumer bankruptcy attorney can often help you come up with a plan to keep your important possessions. But you can't wait until it is too late. If you feel like things are slipping and you can't keep up with your bills, the time to act is now. At our initial consultation, we will evaluate your situation and help come up with the best option available. Whether we help to eliminate your debt through a Chapter 7 bankruptcy or help come up with a personal reorganization plan using a Chapter 13 bankruptcy, all will be done pursuant to federal law and under the supervision of a federal bankruptcy judge.

This is a good time to explore the difference between secured and unsecured debts, as explained by Attorney Joshua Lawhorn.

Secured and Unsecured Debts: What's the Difference?
By Attorney Joshua Lawhorn

A frequent topic of discussion in the initial consultation is the difference between secured and unsecured debt. While the difference is fairly easy to understand, the way in which the debts are treated can be complex.

On its most basic level, a debt is secured when you provide property as collateral for the debt. The lender then has a "lien" on that property. Once the lien is created, the lender can get the property back if you fall behind on loan payments. If the secured loan is a mortgage, the lender could take your home through a foreclosure.

The most common forms of secured debts are car loans, mortgages, and personal property loans. While secured loans are usually an agreement between you and the lender, debts such as tax liens can become secured without your consent.

An unsecured debt is a debt that is not secured by collateral. The most common forms of unsecured debts are credit cards, medical bills, signature loans, and student loans. Usually, a lender collects on unsecured debt by filing a lawsuit against you and asking the court for the right to garnish your wages or bank account balances.

Secured and unsecured debts are treated differently in a Chapter 7 bankruptcy case and in a Chapter 13 reorganization. In Chapter 7 cases, most unsecured debts are dischargeable, while a secured debt would not be if you want to keep the collateral. In a Chapter 13 reorganization, you must pay the secured debt to keep the property that was pledged as collateral. However, you may only have to pay a portion of your unsecured debt. In some cases, you may not have to pay any of the unsecured debt.

While the difference between secured and unsecured debt is fairly simple, the way each debt is treated can be quite complex. For this very reason, it is essential that you speak with an experienced attorney to know your rights regardless of what type of debt you owe.

Attorney Amy Tanner comments on the current exemptions available to citizens throughout the Unites States.

Is Your Home State Allowing Debt Collectors to Leave You in Poverty?
By Attorney Amy K. Tanner

The National Consumer Law Center (NCLC) has recently surveyed the exemption laws of all fifty states, the District of Columbia, Puerto Rico, and the Virgin Islands. What NCLC found is that not even one jurisdiction's exemption laws meet basic standards of living that would allow a debtor to continue to support themselves and their family.

State exemption laws have become outdated, and new legislation is not being brought or passed to bring the exemptions up to date with the current economy. The NCLC reports that in 2012 debt buyers purchased consumer accounts with an aggregate face value of $143 billion dollars for pennies on the dollar, according to the Federal Trade Commission, and much of this debt is unverifiable. States can prevent these debt buyers from leaving families in poverty if each state/jurisdiction will simply update its exemption laws.

The NCLC has made recommendations for reformation of state exemption laws. The NCLC has suggested that the laws should protect a working car, work tools and equipment, money for commuting and other daily work expenses. The law should also protect the family home, necessary household goods, and means of transportation. The NCLC also suggests the laws protect a living wage for working debtors to meet basic needs and protect, at minimum, $1,200 in a bank account for utility bills, etc. The law should further protect retirees by restricting the ability of creditors to seize pensions and retirement incomes and should have built-in updates for inflation. The NCLC also recommends that the law be self-enforcing to ensure that a debtor will not have to file complicated and costly paperwork or take time away from work to attend hearings.

These are all good recommendation that would certainly be welcome by debtors in all jurisdictions. If you are being pursued by a debt collector or are under any financial stress at this time, please contact our office nearest you to schedule a free consultation with one of our attorneys to discuss your situation and tell us what we can do for you.

Disclosure of assets in a bankruptcy filing is not only a good idea, it is a mandatory requirement. Bankruptcy case law often quotes the tenet that bankruptcy relief is available to the honest debtor. Bankruptcy law mandates and requires that everyone is absolutely honest about the property and assets that they do own, and the Bankruptcy Code requires full disclosure of all property and assets in the filing of a bankruptcy case. Attorney Joshua Lawhorn speaks to this:

How Do You Disclose Assets When Filing for Bankruptcy?
By Attorney Joshua Lawhorn

When you seek relief through Chapter 13 personal reorganization or Chapter 7 bankruptcy, you are required to disclose your income and your assets. Disclosing your income is usually quite simple. For most people, you simply provide copies of your pay stubs for the past six months and your bank statements for the past three months. If you are self-employed, our office has forms to help you break down your personal income in a simple and concise manner.

The main question my clients usually have is how to disclose their assets. The court asks that you disclose assets such as furniture, clothing, tools, televisions, and vehicles. The confusion usually doesn't occur with what to disclose, but how to place a value on it. The value should be what you could get for the item if you sold it, not the replacement cost of a brand-new item. There is no need to over think this process. Vehicles are usually easy to valuate due to online resources that provide a value after you enter simple information.

The primary thing to remember is to be honest. Recently, the trustee assigned to new reality star Todd Chrisley's bankruptcy case alleged that he was not completely truthful when disclosing his assets. It wasn't the fact that Chrisley stated his clothes were worth $650.00 that caused the trustee to take action; it was later statements that got Chrisley in hot water. On his reality show, he apparently states that they spend hundreds of thousands of dollars just on clothing. This clearly contradicts his valuation that he provided the court under oath. Chrisley responds to this inconsistency with the idea that there is a limited market on used men's clothing. While this could very well be true, that is still a large gap between his valuation and his statement, which he knew would be aired on live television.

Again, the best way to avoid any kind of misunderstanding with the trustee is to be truthful. Also, our experienced attorneys can help with any question that you have while you go through this process. There is no need for you to go through this alone, and it is not advisable that you do so.

Attorney Amy Tanner comments on the mandatory disclosure of a personal injury or tort claim in the bankruptcy petition prior to the bankruptcy petition being filed. The law provides for harsh results for the unfortunate debtor who does not disclose a potential claim or cause of action of any type in his or her bankruptcy case.

Do I Have to Tell My Bankruptcy Lawyer About My Personal Injury Lawsuit?

By Attorney Amy K. Tanner

The simple and emphatic answer to this is yes! At the time that you file your bankruptcy petition, either Chapter 7 or Chapter 13, you must list any pending lawsuits or potential claims that you may have stemming from any incident existing at that time, even if you have not yet retained a lawyer to handle it. It is also very important to notify your personal injury attorney that you have filed a bankruptcy as there are several motions that will need to be filed in your bankruptcy case in order for you to continue to pursue your personal injury claim. The Bankruptcy Trustee will also work closely with this attorney to administer this asset through your Chapter 13 or Chapter 7 bankruptcy. Failure to disclose a personal injury claim or any other type of claim that you may have will most likely result in you NOT being able to pursue your claim under the legal concept called *collateral estoppel.*

What if something happens after your bankruptcy case is filed that were to give you a cause of action for a personal injury suit against someone or some entity? You must contact your bankruptcy attorney and provide the information so that your bankruptcy petition and schedules can be amended to disclose the action. If you do not disclose any potential claim that arises either pre- bankruptcy filing or post-bankruptcy filing, you will lose the right to pursue that claim or, in plainer terms, you will lose the right to any recovery from that suit for your benefit. This again is the collateral estoppel doctrine.

What happens with the proceeds from the personal injury or lawsuit claim? First of all, these proceeds will be distributed through your bankruptcy estate for the benefit of your unsecured creditors. Once all creditors, fees, and costs of the bankruptcy estate have been paid in full, the debtor will receive any remaining proceeds from the claim.

If you are experiencing problems with multiple creditors, there can actually be some benefit to filing a bankruptcy while you are awaiting resolution of a personal injury claim. The filing of the bankruptcy can stop creditor harassment while you focus on your pending litigation. You may also be able to pay less to your creditors through the administration of a bankruptcy estate than if you received the proceeds of a lawsuit and tried to navigate paying all of your creditors directly, on your own.

Amy also comments on the event that assets come into the bankruptcy case during the bankruptcy itself.

What if I Win the Lottery (or Other Possible Windfalls) Before, During, or After My Bankruptcy?
By Attorney Amy K. Tanner

The odds of actually winning the lottery are, unfortunately, pretty slim! The chances, however, are greater that, after seeking bankruptcy protection, you may find yourself the recipient of some type of windfall. This can come in the form of an inheritance, a property settlement as a result of a divorce, sale of real estate, receipt of proceeds from a life insurance policy, proceeds from a personal injury claim or any other kind of lawsuit proceeds, and, yes, lottery or gambling winnings.

At the time that you file your bankruptcy petition, whether it is a Chapter 7 or Chapter 13, it is imperative that you **list any and all** of these as potential assets if, at the time you file, you have reason to believe you will receive a windfall of any kind. If you are unaware at the time of filing, then it is very important to let your bankruptcy attorney know immediately if it becomes apparent to you that you will be receiving funds in addition to your normal monthly income.

If you have a windfall anytime during the life of your Chapter 13 payment plan, the proceeds will go toward paying your creditors through the Chapter 13 plan. This can sometimes pay your case out early, and you will receive an early discharge.

Some final comments and thoughts before we leave this chapter. Since we have just discussed that it is mandatory that all assets and property and potential claims and assets be disclosed in a bankruptcy filing, a common question that many of our clients have is whether they can transfer or give some of their property to someone else so that they do not take the chance of losing it. Our answer to that question is an emphatic no!

Can I Transfer or Give Away Any of My Property Before I File for Bankruptcy? By Attorney Ronald C. Sykstus

A common question that we are often asked is whether someone can give away or transfer over property in order to avoid their creditors if they are going to file for bankruptcy. The very short and quick answer is **no**. While it may sound like a good idea on the surface, federal bankruptcy law and most states have enacted laws which strictly prohibit a debtor (someone who is filing for bankruptcy) from doing this. We always advise our clients to, using a golf analogy, play the ball as it lies. That means, in essence, to not make any transfers or changes to any of your property in contemplation of a bankruptcy filing.

Of course, if there will **never** be a bankruptcy filing, then transfers or changes to property are acceptable. The context in which we see this issue, however, is when a client comes to us and has property in their name that is not exempt for bankruptcy purposes and they want to save it by giving it to a family member or friend. The answer to whether someone should do this is an **absolute no**. Exemption planning can be very tricky and problematic in this context. The federal bankruptcy laws are very generous to people who are honest about their dealings with their property and their debts. As a result, when someone comes to us, no matter what their situation is, we essentially tell them to freeze everything, meaning do not make any changes to property, either giving any of their property away or adding to their property.

This can be a big problem under the federal bankruptcy laws. In light of the fact that the bankruptcy laws require full and complete disclosure of the entire financial picture of the person who is filing, absolute honesty is an absolute requirement. It is a must when someone is filing for bankruptcy. Failure to disclose transfers of property can result in denial of a bankruptcy discharge and, at its worst, criminal charges. Full disclosure of transfers prior to filing for bankruptcy can obviously result in the bankruptcy court and trustee voiding out the transfer and seizing back the property. The bankruptcy laws fully address this and most states have also enacted fraudulent conveyance statutes to address this exact situation. The fraudulent conveyance statute that almost all states have can be utilized by a bankruptcy trustee in order to go after and try to void out transfers that were made, especially to insiders (defined as immediate family members) going back the last ten years.

The simple example is a parent who deeds over a paid-for house to a child without receiving adequate payment or consideration. The parent then attempts to try to file for bankruptcy. The transfer must be disclosed in the bankruptcy petition since an "insider," defined as an immediate family member, was involved and adequate consideration was not paid for the transfer. Suffice it to say as it relates to the transferring of assets, the longer the better, and by longer for substantial assets, ten years or more is the magic mark as far as the time between the transfer of the asset and the subsequent bankruptcy filing.

Our advice is to tread very cautiously when and if someone is thinking about transferring property prior to a bankruptcy filing. Before you do anything like this, it is best to get a full and complete understanding of your situation. Therefore, we advise sitting down with one of our licensed attorneys in a confidential setting to discuss all of your options.

Attorney Mary Pool offers commentary in a detailed fashion on the law that applies here with regard to the transfer of property.

What Is the Bankruptcy 90-Day Rule?
By Attorney Mary Conner Pool

If you have transferred property or money to a creditor within 90 days or an insider (i.e., relative or friend) within a year of your bankruptcy filing, you should be aware of the 90-day bankruptcy rule. It is crucial that you discuss any transfers of property that you have made with your bankruptcy attorney so that you may protect any meaningful transfers you have made.

The bankruptcy 90-day rule relates to the debts that a filer has paid in the last 90 days prior to their bankruptcy filing. Section 547(b) of the Bankruptcy Code establishes the parameters of the 90-day rule:

"... the trustee may avoid any transfer of an interest of the debtor in property –

(1) To or for the benefit of a creditor;

(2) For or on account of an antecedent debt owed by the debtor before such transfer was made;

(3) Made while the debtor was insolvent;

(4) Made –

(A) on or within 90 days before the date of the filing of the petition; or

(B) between 90 days and one year before the date of the filing of the petition, if such a creditor at the time of such transfer was an insider; and

(5) That enables such creditor to receive more than such creditor would receive if –

(A) the case were a case under Chapter 7 of this title..." unless the amount was for less than $600 (see section 547(c)(8)).

What does this mean? It means that the trustee may avoid a transfer made to a creditor and/or insider if you have transferred any property that has an aggregate value of <u>$600 or more</u>, and

1. **the transfer was made within 90 days of your bankruptcy filing, or**
2. **the transfer was made within 90 days to one year if the creditor is an insider (i.e., relative or friend).**

Example 1: John wanted to try to settle his debts before filing bankruptcy. He had saved about $5,000 to help him negotiate with his creditors. He was successful in settling only two of his debts and paid $600 on July 30, 2013 to Company A and $4,400 on August 5, 2013 to Company B. After negotiating these settlements he was unsuccessful in settling any of his other debts, so he filed Chapter 7 on August 15, 2013. Since John paid $600 to Company A, and more than $600 to Company B, the trustee may seek to avoid these transfers and get the money back. This will allow all John's creditors to receive an equal share of the funds and prevent one particular creditor from benefiting more than others.

The second part of the rule allows the bankruptcy trustee to avoid any transfers of property made to any creditor who is also an insider (i.e., relative or friend) made between 90 days and one year of your bankruptcy filing date and exceeds an aggregate value of $600 or more.

Example 2: Sarah bought her daughter Kim a car for graduating college and paid $16,000 from funds she kept in her savings account. After buying the car, she transferred the title to her daughter on May 20, 2013, as a gift for her graduation. In July 2013, Sarah lost her job and was unable to pay her debts due to her only receiving unemployment income. After four months with no job, Sarah decided to file Chapter 7 to receive a fresh financial start. If Sarah were to file for bankruptcy prior to May 21, 2014, the trustee would be able to avoid the title transfer she made to her daughter. This would put the vehicle she purchased for her daughter at risk. It is important for Sarah to be warned about this risk prior to her filing bankruptcy. If her bankruptcy attorney was made aware of this fact, he/she would have warned Sarah prior to her filing for Chapter 7.

Keep in mind that the rule involves all property, not just cash. There are some exceptions to this rule, including if property was transferred in the ordinary course of business (i.e., the property was sold and the value you received was a fair and accurate value of the property). Also, this rule applies to both a Chapter 7 and Chapter 13.

Chapter 10

Time Limits Between Bankruptcy Filings

For an initial bankruptcy filing, where the individual or couple has never filed a bankruptcy before, time limits are obviously meaningless as far as previous filings. Due to the dramatic change in the bankruptcy law in 2005, however, time limits between bankruptcy filings are now a very big deal in the unfortunate case that a person or couple has to contemplate debt solutions after a bankruptcy has been filed in their past. Attorney Amy Tanner has written a series of articles on time limits and timing of subsequent bankruptcy filings.

Time Limits of BK
When Can I File Bankruptcy Again?
By Attorney Amy K. Tanner

Despite what most people think, considering the current economy, bankruptcy filings are actually down nationwide. One would think that with the high rate of foreclosures, job losses, sequestration, and cutbacks that more people would have a need to file bankruptcy. It seems that during an economic recession, Americans begin to feel so down and out that even seeking much-needed bankruptcy assistance is just too burdensome.

However, one factor in the declining number of bankruptcy filings may stem back to the dramatic change in the bankruptcy law in 2005. In the few months and weeks leading up to the October 15, 2005 effective date of the current bankruptcy law, many people flocked to bankruptcy practitioners nationwide in fear that this new bankruptcy law would make it harder or impossible to file after it took effect. One of the notable changes in the new law set a time limitation of eight years between consecutive Chapter 7 bankruptcy filings. The old law placed a limit of only six years between consecutive Chapter 7 bankruptcy filings.

I am fairly certain that many people who filed just before the law changed in October 2005 may not even have needed to file as badly as they assumed as the economy was pretty good back then. Since that time, we, as a country, have gone into an economic recession. Some of the people who filed on the eve of the change in the law have suffered through job losses, foreclosures, and other economic hardships, but have been ineligible to seek bankruptcy help due to a previous filing.

Many folks who filed out of fear of losing the right to file may be in need of assistance again, and this is all right. I believe that when folks realize that they are able to file again, we will see a rise in the numbers of bankruptcy filings nationwide. This is not a bad thing; it will be a very good thing for those who have been suffering through economic hardship over the last few years.

Can I File a Chapter 13 Debt Consolidation Bankruptcy After I Have Received a Chapter 7 Discharge?
By Attorney Amy K. Tanner

There are certain time limitations on filing repeated bankruptcies. **However, there is almost never a time that you cannot file a Chapter 13 bankruptcy if you are facing a financial hardship and need the benefit of the automatic stay in order to stop your creditors from pursuing you with garnishments, foreclosure, repossession, or other harassing collection efforts.**

If you have filed a Chapter 7 bankruptcy and received a discharge, you cannot file another Chapter 7 bankruptcy for which you can receive a discharge for eight years from the date of filing the first Chapter 7. Therefore, it is not feasible to file a Chapter 7 at all within that eight-year period.

If you have filed a Chapter 7 bankruptcy for which you have received a discharge, you can file a Chapter 13 debt consolidation four years from the date of the filing of the Chapter 7.

Some of the other time limitations on filing repeat bankruptcies are times between Chapter 13 filings. If you initially filed a Chapter 13 and received a discharge, you must wait only two years to file another Chapter 13 or, if you need a total fresh start, you need only wait six years from the time of filing a Chapter 13 from which you received a discharge to file a Chapter 7.

There are some other intricacies of time limitations based upon whether or not you converted a previous bankruptcy case from one chapter to another or whether or not you received a discharge.

These limitations can seem confusing to navigate. If you are being harassed by your creditors or are facing a foreclosure, repossession, and/or a garnishment and you are afraid that you cannot file a bankruptcy for relief because you have filed one before, please contact one of our offices nearest to you as there is almost never a time that you cannot get some type of relief in bankruptcy.

Can I File for Bankruptcy Again? ...and Again? ...and Again...?
By Attorney Amy K. Tanner

A question we are asked repeatedly is whether a person can file bankruptcy after previously filing for bankruptcy. The question is an important one at this time due to the eight-year anniversary of the most dramatic change to bankruptcy law in the last 25 years. On October 17, 2005, the new bankruptcy law, often referred to as BAPCPA, was enacted, which, in essence, put a lot more burden on individuals trying to file for bankruptcy and get a fresh start. Among the many changes was one of time limitations between bankruptcy filings.

In the few months and weeks leading up to the October 17, 2005 effective date of this new bankruptcy law, many people flocked to bankruptcy attorneys nationwide in fear that this new bankruptcy law would make it harder or impossible to file after it took effect. One of the most notable changes in the new law is that it set a time limitation of eight years between consecutive Chapter 7 bankruptcy filings.

Our attorneys are well versed in the bankruptcy filing timelines and in all aspects of bankruptcy law and practice. This includes knowing and understanding time limitations between both Chapter 7 straight bankruptcy filings and Chapter 13 debt consolidation filings.

Chapter 11

Should I File for Bankruptcy? If So, What Type Should I File and How Can It Help Me?

The title of this chapter is really a misnomer. The answer is, at least right now, that we don't know and you don't know. As discussed previously, you should really review your entire situation with an objective attorney to determine what, if any, course of action you should take. With that said, this chapter will deal with the broad generalities of whether a person should file for bankruptcy, what type, and how a person can be helped through bankruptcy. There are more nuanced areas of bankruptcy that we will deal with in the next chapter.

Is It Time for You to Consider Filing For Bankruptcy?
By Attorney Bradford W. Botes

Many people are unable to pay their bills as they become due but clearly not all of them are candidates for bankruptcy. So when should an individual consider filing for bankruptcy? The truth is that there is no bright line to help make this determination. Each person's situation is different. Here, however, are some of the factors that should be considered in making this determination:

Are you only able to make minimum monthly payments on your credit card bills?

If the answer is yes, then you may be on a treadmill that will be difficult to get off. Minimum payments often cover only the interest that has accrued in the last month and a little bit more. It could take many years for you to pay off what you owe.

Do you have property or belongings that might be lost if you file bankruptcy?

The amount of property that you are able to retain, or claim as exempt, in bankruptcy varies from state to state and should be discussed with a bankruptcy attorney in your area. If, however, you own very little or owe more on what you do own than what it is worth, then it is likely that you would not lose anything if you filed. Even if you do own property that has significant value, there are types of bankruptcy that may allow you to keep what you own.

How much do you owe?

It is not necessary that you owe any certain amount to seek bankruptcy protection. For some people, $100,000 may be too much debt. For others, it may be as little as $5,000. How much is too much for any one individual depends upon that person's circumstances. How much you earn, together with the type of debt you owe, are two of many factors that should be considered.

Are you facing a foreclosure, wage garnishment, or repossession?

If the answer to any of these is yes, then your finances are likely already at a point at which you should consult with an attorney. Losing your home, your car, or your wages could be devastating. Bankruptcy protection may be able to stop this from happening. You need to know your options.

How much stress can you deal with?

For many people, the anxiety caused by juggling bills, answering calls from collectors, and opening letters demanding payment can be overwhelming. The resulting stress can cause loss of sleep, an inability to perform one's job, and tension amongst loved ones. Money problems are at the root of many failed marriages.

The factors above do not need to be considered alone. If you are having difficulty paying your bills, you owe it to yourself to learn all of your options. Don't let either fear or pride keep you from seeking help.

If a person is considering a possible bankruptcy filing, then the question is what type? Attorney Grant McNutt addresses this.

Should I File a Chapter 13 Bankruptcy or a Chapter 7 Bankruptcy? By Attorney Grant McNutt

When most people think about bankruptcy, they think about it in terms of Chapter 7 or "straight bankruptcy" when you just "wipe out" or discharge debts. This fresh start sounds nice; however, this is not always the best answer for many reasons. If it is not the best answer, then should you file a Chapter 13 debt consolidation? Filing a Chapter 13 debt consolidation can help you resolve many issues. It can usually be filed with the court in a matter of days from the first time you meet with an attorney, thereby relieving you of creditor harassment almost immediately in addition to stopping garnishments, lawsuits, repossessions, and foreclosures. It may also be beneficial in actually lowering your monthly outgo of expenses.

Another issue most people don't consider in the process of making the choice between filing Chapter 7 or Chapter 13 is whether they have health insurance. One concern with filing a Chapter 7 bankruptcy is that it may prevent you from declaring bankruptcy or being eligible for another bankruptcy discharge for a longer period of time. If you currently have no health insurance, filing a Chapter 7 could be perilous to your financial future. If you were to suffer an accident or some other medical problem and you are not insured, you will most likely have some enormous medical bills. If you filed a Chapter 7 previously, you would be barred from bankruptcy relief for a longer period of time and would more or less be suffering collection harassment and possible garnishment from medical bills that you could not get relief from because of the Chapter 7 you filed. This is a valid issue and an issue that is not often discussed; however, it is one that I and the other attorneys here at Bond and Botes do consider when advising our clients, as we want to help you choose the best option to afford you the most long-term financial help and relief.

Attorney Cynthia Lawson addresses five myths about bankruptcy.

Five Myths About Bankruptcy
By Attorney Cynthia T. Lawson

Myth #1: I can never get credit again

Filing a bankruptcy is on your credit report for ten years; however, just because a bankruptcy is being reported on your credit report doesn't mean you can never get credit. Usually as soon as you receive a discharge in bankruptcy, you are eligible for loans, and in fact many subprime lenders solicit newly discharged debtors for high-interest credit cards and signature loans because the creditor knows a Chapter 7 can only be filed once every eight years.

Myth #2: I am going to lose my home

All states and the federal law allow persons filing a bankruptcy to protect a certain amount of equity in the home (equity is the difference between what the home is worth and what you owe on it). The federal government allows individuals who can't claim a state's exemption to protect $250,000 of equity in a home. Tennessee allows between $5,000 and $50,000 depending on age and whether you have minor children or custody of a minor child. Alabama's homestead exemption is up to $5,000 and Mississippi's exemption is up to $75,000. Even if your attorney believes you have too much equity to protect or exempt, a Chapter 13 may allow you to reduce your debt and still protect your home.

Myth #3: I will lose my vehicle, car, boat, truck, or motorcycle if I file bankruptcy

Generally, as long as you are current on your vehicle loan, and you don't have a lot of equity, your vehicle can be protected if you file a Chapter 7 bankruptcy. If you are behind on payments or have a lot of equity in your vehicle, a Chapter 13 can reduce the interest rate, monthly payment, and allow you to cure what you are behind on the vehicle loan.

Myth #4: I don't have to list my medical bills in my bankruptcy or you can't list medical bills in a bankruptcy

All debts must be listed in a bankruptcy, including medical bills; usually all medical bills are discharged in a bankruptcy. In a Chapter 7 you can voluntarily pay back your favorite doctor if you want to, even after you have discharged that doctor in your bankruptcy. In a Chapter 13 the hospital or doctor will receive whatever you can afford to pay on the medical bill. A hospital receiving federal money cannot refuse you service just because you listed the hospital in your bankruptcy.

Myth #5: I can't discharge a utility bill in bankruptcy

All debts are listed in a bankruptcy filing, so if you are behind on a utility bill, it must be included in the bankruptcy. If your utility company is the only service provider available to you, which most are, the utility company cannot turn off service because you filed their debt in the bankruptcy. The utility company can only require that you pay another reconnection fee and/or security deposit to keep your service from being interrupted. Be sure to tell your attorney if you are behind on a utility bill when you meet with them.

A final issue to address here are the qualifications for bankruptcy. Specifically, does a person have to have a certain amount of debt before he or she qualifies for bankruptcy? Can a person owe too much debt and still qualify for bankruptcy? How much debt should a person have before a bankruptcy is filed? All of these questions are really a case-by-case decision with a person considering the bankruptcy filing with his or her attorney. Attorney Amy Tanner addresses these concerns.

Do I Owe Enough to File for Bankruptcy? (Or Too Much?!)
By Attorney Amy K. Tanner

Do I owe enough to file for bankruptcy? This is a question that my colleagues and I hear quite often. My initial response is the amount of debt you owe is relative to your financial situation. Many people feel overwhelmed by debt but are concerned that they don't owe enough to consider bankruptcy as an option. However, in many instances a person's credit has been so marred by the bad debts that a bankruptcy filing is a much quicker and less stressful avenue to getting back to a good credit rating. Of course, there is an element of logic or feasibility in determining if your debts are too few or too small to choose a bankruptcy option. There are many reasons to file some form of bankruptcy even if your total amount of debt is small. You may be in fear of garnishment of your wages, repossession, or judgments. A bankruptcy can stop these collection efforts and keep your wages under your control and in your pocket.

Some potential bankruptcy filers may also question if they owe too much to file for bankruptcy. The simple answer to this questions is no. However, there are certain debt limits for filing a Chapter 13 consumer debt consolidation bankruptcy. In order to confirm a Chapter 13 debt consolidation, you cannot include in excess of $383,175 in unsecured debt (credit cards, medical bills, signature loans, etc.) and $1,149,525 in secured debts (debts with collateral). Please note that these limitations are effective as of this publication, and the debt limits increase generally once or twice per year. If you exceed these debt limits, don't be discouraged. There are other alternatives to consider. A better option may be a Chapter 7 bankruptcy or fresh start bankruptcy or an "individual" Chapter 11 (reorganization/debt consolidation) bankruptcy.

Chapter 12

Bankruptcy Concepts and Issues

A. Credit Counseling and Financial Management/Debtor Education Requirements

For every bankruptcy case that is filed, a debtor must first complete required credit counseling. This requirement came into being when the dramatic change in law occurred in 2005. A person who wants to file bankruptcy has to first obtain a certificate of credit counseling after having attended an approved course. This certificate must be filed at the time that the bankruptcy is filed or the bankruptcy will be null and void. Every bankruptcy court in the country provides a list of approved credit counseling organizations at the bankruptcy court's website. This is not a long process and people can get through the credit counseling course quickly.

There is a subsequent requirement while the bankruptcy is ongoing for the debtor to attend and complete a personal financial management class, also referred to as debtor education. This class must be completed and a certificate of completion must be filed with the bankruptcy court prior to a discharge being entered. This is another mandatory requirement put in place under the bankruptcy law changes in 2005. While we recommend all debtor education courses as approved by our local bankruptcy courts in which we practice, we highlight Dave Ramsey's course. His slogan is "The course may be mandatory, but boring is optional." Our clients receive a book entitled *Starting Over*—Dave Ramsey's Post Bankruptcy Survival Guide, used in his starting over course. We recommend this one because it promotes a change in life and reduction in debt stress. Dave Ramsey's organization wants this to be a change of life—so do we! We hope you never need to be a bankruptcy client again!

B. What Happens at a Meeting with a Bankruptcy Attorney?

What Happens at a Meeting With a Bankruptcy Attorney?
By Attorney Bradford W. Botes

Although it may be in their best interest to do so, people avoid meeting with bankruptcy attorneys. Folks who do come in to see us often tell us that they put off doing so for days, weeks, or even months. In many cases, we could have done a lot more to help them if they had come in earlier. Our clients tell us that they were embarrassed about calling our office to schedule an appointment. They felt like it meant they were a failure. Most felt that if they had just waited a little bit longer, things would get better. Instead, things often got worse.

If you are having financial problems, if the stress of dealing with creditors is affecting your marriage, if a creditor is suing you or garnishing your wages, or if you are facing a foreclosure, you owe it to yourself to explore all of your options. In most cases, meeting face-to-face with a local professional attorney who is experienced in helping people with money problems will be your best option. As my law partner Carla Handy has pointed out, dealing with an out-of-state company at the opposite end of a toll-free number can be risky.

So what happens when you meet with a bankruptcy attorney? We have offices in Alabama, Mississippi, and Tennessee. In each office, we offer a free personal and confidential consultation with one of our experienced attorneys. You will not meet with a secretary or paralegal. Prior to the meeting, you will be asked to complete a simple form with some basic information that we will use to evaluate your circumstances. You can even download and complete the form before your appointment.

During the consultation, we will meet and get to know each other. It may surprise you that our first objective will be to keep you out of bankruptcy. In addition to bankruptcy, our firm can help with lawsuit defense, credit report disputes, and dealing with abusive collectors. All options will be explored. After reviewing your assets, liabilities, income, and expenses, we will answer your questions and help you make the best decision possible. If you determine that you want to retain us to file bankruptcy or take some other action on your behalf, we will quote you a fair fee and then allow you to make a pressure-free decision.

In short, if we do our job correctly, you will leave your consultation fully understanding all of your options and prepared to take the first step toward dealing with your problems. If you are dealing with financial problems, please don't allow a stranger to influence your important financial situations. Schedule a free personal and confidential consultation with one of our experienced attorneys. We will do all that we can to help you.

C. The Automatic Stay

The Automatic Stay
By Attorney Bradford W. Botes

In my opinion, no attorney can provide a consumer with more relief, more quickly, than a bankruptcy attorney. On the day a bankruptcy petition is filed, in fact at the very moment the petition is filed, the bankruptcy court enters an order called an automatic stay. The order is entered pursuant to the provisions of Section 362 of Title 11 of the United States Code. It constitutes a directive by a federal judge to each and every creditor of the consumer to immediately stop any and all collection activities. This means that the creditor(s) must cease collection calls, collection letters, lawsuits, garnishments, and even foreclosure proceedings.

We often have folks come into our office who have gotten behind on their bills and are facing relentless collection calls from their creditors. The collectors can be belligerent and cause a lot of stress for the person on the receiving end of the calls. The stress can cause health problems and put pressure upon a marriage. By filing a bankruptcy petition, we can immediately stop the calls.

Others may come to see us who have gotten behind on their mortgage payments and are facing a potential foreclosure. In many states—including Alabama, Mississippi, and Tennessee—the foreclosure process can take place very quickly. Losing a family home can have a devastating effect on a family. Filing a bankruptcy petition, even one hour before a foreclosure sale, although it's not advisable to wait until the eleventh hour, will stop the sale and give the homeowner a chance to save their home.

If an individual who comes to see us is facing a lawsuit or even a garnishment, a bankruptcy filing will immediately stop the collector's efforts to garnish the person's wages or bank account. In certain circumstances, we may even be able to get back some of the money that has already been garnished.

Many people are facing financial problems in today's economy. If you are one of them, please consult face-to-face with an experienced bankruptcy attorney so that you can learn your options. The automatic stay may be the time out that you need in order to get your life back on track.

What Is the Automatic Stay in Bankruptcy?
By Attorney Amy K. Tanner

Technically, the provision for the automatic stay that applies to every bankruptcy case that is filed is found in 11 USC §362. This is the United States Bankruptcy Code. The practical effect, however, of the automatic stay is of utmost importance to anyone seeking relief from creditor harassment, repossession of personal property, or foreclosure of real property. This provides a huge relief to people who file for any chapter of relief under the Bankruptcy Code.

Upon the exact minute of the filing of a bankruptcy petition with the bankruptcy court, this automatic stay goes into immediate effect and is applicable to all creditors. This will give a person who files immediate relief from the incessant creditor phone calls and relieve them from fear of an automobile being repossessed or a home being foreclosed upon as it prevents any action by creditors to collect on a debt. Once the automatic stay has gone into effect, all creditors of the bankruptcy petitioner must immediately cease any type of collection efforts against the debtor directly. The creditors must handle the majority of post-bankruptcy matters either through the attorney of record and/or by filing a formal motion to be set for hearing before the bankruptcy court. The automatic stay is the exact type of relief intended by the bankruptcy law to relieve a debtor of financial stress.

D. If I Am Considering Filing for Bankruptcy and I Am Married, Am I Required to File Bankruptcy with My Spouse?

The issue for many married people considering bankruptcy is whether to file a joint case with their spouse or an individual case. You are not required to file a joint bankruptcy petition just because you are married. In most traditional marriage situations, there is a good bit of joint debt, or both spouses already suffer from problem credit. A joint filing in this instance is usually the most economical household decision to make. However, many married couples today keep their finances and their debts completely separate, or one spouse may have premarital debt and bad credit and would like to get into a better situation to move forward in their married life. These circumstances may warrant an individual bankruptcy filing and not including the current spouse.

Filing a bankruptcy petition is a personal decision and, in a marriage, oftentimes a bankruptcy filing can alleviate marital stress brought on by financial problems. It is helpful for a married couple to seek the counsel of an experienced bankruptcy attorney to help them make this important decision.

E. What Is a Bankruptcy Trustee?

What Is a Bankruptcy Trustee?
By Attorney Grant McNutt

Every consumer bankruptcy case that is filed, both Chapter 13 and Chapter 7, is assigned to a trustee. The trustee is in charge of the administration of the bankruptcy estate. A bankruptcy trustee is usually either an attorney or a certified public accountant who has been appointed to the position of trustee.

A person who has filed a consumer bankruptcy will first meet his/her trustee at the initial hearing or §341 meeting of creditors. It is called the §341 meeting as this is the section of the Bankruptcy Code that mandates this hearing. The trustee or a representative of the trustee will conduct the hearing.

One of the primary duties of a bankruptcy trustee is to insure that creditors are being treated fairly. In a Chapter 7 or "liquidation" bankruptcy, it is the trustee's job to review a debtor's bankruptcy petition and schedules to determine if there are any assets above a debtor's allowed exemptions that could be liquidated in order to generate funds to pay the unsecured creditors. In a Chapter 13 or debt consolidation bankruptcy, the trustee receives the debtor's Chapter 13 plan payments every month and, in turn, will distribute the payments proportionally to all claims that have been timely filed by creditors in the case. The trustee will also review a debtor's petition and schedules to insure that the debtor is paying all of her disposable income into the Chapter 13 plan, thereby making certain that the creditors are receiving all that the debtor can afford to pay. The Chapter 13 trustee will act on behalf of a debtor to insure that both the debtor and the creditors are treated fairly. Most attorneys work very closely with the district's trustees to assist clients in getting through the complicated bankruptcy process.

F. Can I Be Denied a Bankruptcy Discharge from My Debts?

Can I Be Denied a Bankruptcy Discharge from My Debts?
By Attorney Cynthia Lawson

Yes, you can be denied a bankruptcy discharge, but this is a rare occurrence. The most common occurrence is when a debtor has committed a fairly serious fraud against his creditors. A more common occurrence, but still rare, is being denied a discharge of a single debt for various legal reasons. There are a few sections of the Bankruptcy Code that discuss the discharge in general or discharge of certain debts. These sections can be found at 11 U.S.C. §523 and 11 U.S.C. §727.

Some of the common debts that can be denied a discharge include debts that are incurred within 90 days of the filing of a bankruptcy that are in excess of $500 and obtained for luxury goods or services, cash advances aggregating more than $750 that are extensions of consumer credit under an open-end credit plan obtained by an individual debtor on or within 70 days before the order for relief under this title are presumed to be non-dischargeable. These issues usually arise in a Chapter 7 and most always result in only the questionable debt being determined non-dischargeable.

On more rare occasions, a debtor may be denied a discharge of his entire case for more serious offenses that include fraudulent transfers prior to the filing of a bankruptcy, false or untrue information in the filed bankruptcy schedules, and hiding assets with intent to defraud creditors. These are a few of the more serious issues that will lead to eventual denial of a bankruptcy discharge.

In addition, a debtor can also be denied a discharge of the entire case if the debtor, or joint debtors, fail to complete a post-petition financial management course or has received a discharge from a previous bankruptcy within a certain time period. The Bankruptcy Code sets out the financial management requirement as well as the time limitations between bankruptcy discharges.

G. Can I Be Held Responsible for Another Person's Debts Like My Husband/Wife/Parent/Child/Friend?

Can I Be Held Responsible for Another Person's Debts Like My Husband/Wife/Parent/Child/Friend?
By Attorney Ronald C. Sykstus

A common question we are asked is whether a person can be held responsible for another person's debts. The concern most often comes up with regard to a spouse, such as a wife being concerned about responsibility for her husband's debts or vice versa or a parent being responsible for a child's debt or a child being concerned about a parent's debt. The short and simple answer is that no, you cannot be held responsible for another person's debts. This analysis changes, however, if you have signed as a responsible party, either as a co-signer or guarantor on the debt. A simple way to check this is to determine whether or not you signed the contract for the underlying debt with your husband/wife/parent/child/friend. If you have not signed the contract and never had a connection to the debt (also referred to legally as privity of contract), the debt itself does not transfer over to you simply by virtue of the fact that you have a relationship with that person. Debt collectors, however, sometimes will try to deceive one person into believing that they are, in fact, responsible for paying another person's debt even though that party did not sign the underlying contract. If that type of collection harassment is happening to you, make sure to use the Fair Debt Collection Practices Act and put the debt in dispute.

H. How Will Bankruptcy Affect My Bank Account?

How Will Bankruptcy Affect My Bank Account?
By Attorney Carla Handy

The average person who is contemplating bankruptcy relief works hard every day to take care of their family, and a disruption to their bank account can be devastating. Generally speaking, the funds in a bank account can be protected, but there are certain issues regarding bank accounts and the banking industry in general that you will want to be aware of if you are considering filing for bankruptcy.

First, within the bankruptcy process itself, funds in a bank account can be protected by claiming the money in the account from the claims of creditors. An exemption is simply an amount or value of an asset that the law says, no matter what, your creditors cannot reach. If the bank account fits within the amount allowed by law, the funds are safe and a knowledgeable bankruptcy attorney can guide you in claiming this exemption. Second, in preparing to file for bankruptcy relief, if you owe a debt to a bank where you maintain a checking or savings account, you should strongly consider opening a new account with a bank where you do not owe any money prior to filing. This is because a bank can "set off" against your bank account if you owe them money on a debt and that debt has gone unpaid. The set-off could consist of the bank withdrawing a monthly loan payment that is past due from your account. Or, if the bank has obtained a judgment against you for an unpaid loan, it may pull all of the money in your account to satisfy this debt.

There are certain banks that will deny you access to your checking or savings account once you have filed for bankruptcy relief. While this action by the banks is misguided and based upon an incorrect interpretation of the Bankruptcy Code, it can be very distressing for a debtor while the bankruptcy attorney works to straighten out the problem. For this reason, it is best to open a new account with a more accommodating bank prior to filing the bankruptcy. It is very important to ask your bankruptcy attorney **which banks** will freeze your account and give you a problem **even if you don't owe them anything! Do not ignore this important step!**

Finally, if your paycheck or monthly benefit is direct deposited into a bank account that will need to be closed in preparation for a bankruptcy filing, you will need to take quick action to transfer that deposit to any new bank account that you open. With adequate planning, there is no reason why your bank accounts should be adversely affected by the filing for bankruptcy relief.

I. What Is the Presumption of Abuse in a Chapter 7 Bankruptcy?

What Is the Presumption of Abuse in a Chapter 7 Bankruptcy?
By Attorney Mary Conner Pool

My clients often look at me confused when I mention the presumption of abuse to them when we are reviewing their means test. The presumption of abuse guidelines were established in 2005 when Congress enacted the Bankruptcy Abuse Prevention and Consumer Protection Act of 2005 (BAPCPA). One of the primary reasons for this act was to make it more difficult for consumers who made too much money to be able to file a Chapter 7 and walk away from debts that they could have certainly afforded to pay. If a Chapter 7 consumer's means test shows that they make too much money, their case is presumed to be an abuse of the Bankruptcy Code, meaning they might have to file a Chapter 13 instead to allow them to pay some or all of their unsecured debts.

If the presumption of abuse arises in a Chapter 7 case, you may rebut the presumption by providing documentation of special circumstances that enable you to show that you should still be able to receive a Chapter 7 discharge. For example, in some districts, if the presumption of abuse arises due to the consumer receiving a large amount of overtime, but the consumer is no longer receiving overtime and that is documented by their most recent pay stubs, then a consumer may be able to show that they are no longer receiving the amount of income that caused the presumption of abuse to arise.

A consumer only has two choices if they are unable to rebut the presumption of abuse after their case has been filed. They can either dismiss their Chapter 7 case or convert their case to a Chapter 13, allowing them to repay some or all of their creditors.

J. Can I Dismiss My Chapter 7 Bankruptcy If I Change My Mind After Filing?

Can I Dismiss My Chapter 7 Bankruptcy If I Change My Mind After Filing? By Attorney Carla M. Handy

As a bankruptcy attorney, I have often been asked if a Chapter 7 bankruptcy can be dismissed after filing if the client changes his or her mind and decides not to go through with the case. The best answer is maybe, but not likely. Chapter 7 is the liquidation chapter of the Bankruptcy Code. As a result, the Chapter 7 trustee's job is to determine if the debtor in a Chapter 7 has any assets available for liquidation. Where a Chapter 7 debtor desires to dismiss the bankruptcy case after filing because the Chapter 7 trustee is trying to sell an asset the debtor does not want to lose, a motion to dismiss the Chapter 7 petition by the debtor would most likely be hotly contested by the trustee or creditors in the case who could anticipate being paid on their claims from the proceeds of the sale.

Section 707 of the Bankruptcy Code provides that a Chapter 7 case may only be dismissed after a hearing on the issue is conducted by the bankruptcy judge assigned to the case. The court can only dismiss for cause—that means there must be a compelling reason for the dismissal, and simply changing one's mind would likely not be enough to constitute cause for the bankruptcy judge. However, if the debtor owned no assets available for liquidation in the Chapter 7 and presented the court with a good reason, dismissal could well be granted by the bankruptcy judge.

I had a recent example of this in a Chapter 7 that I filed for a married couple. The wife had uncontrollable seizures that required hospitalization after the filing of the Chapter 7 bankruptcy petition. The husband had been laid off from his employment right before the petition was filed and, as a result, lost medical insurance coverage for the family. This resulted in a $40,000 hospital bill that was post-petition and therefore not eligible to be discharged in the Chapter 7 (debt incurred after the filing of a bankruptcy petition is generally not included in the case or available to be discharged).

I filed a motion to dismiss my clients' case because the $40,000 hospital debt would have completely thwarted my clients' ability to obtain a fresh start after the Chapter 7 discharge. The motion to dismiss was granted by the bankruptcy judge because the reason for the dismissal request was sufficient if not compelling, and the clients had no assets available for liquidation. The trustee, therefore, did not object, nor any creditor in the case.

It is important to note that this issue/problem of voluntary dismissal of a case applies to a Chapter 7 bankruptcy. In a Chapter 13 bankruptcy, a debtor has the right to dismiss his or her case at any time in most jurisdictions. There are some possible limitations here but, as a general rule, a debtor can voluntarily dismiss his or her Chapter 13 bankruptcy case at any time.

It is important when considering filing for bankruptcy relief to ask these types of questions of your bankruptcy attorney if you have concerns about these types of issues. No question is ever a bad question to ask. If you are concerned about it, it's important to make your bankruptcy attorney aware of it. Your bankruptcy attorney is there to advise you, including whether or not a petition should be filed given your particular concerns or circumstances.

K. What Is a Chapter 13 Plan?

What Is a Chapter 13 Plan?
By Attorney Mary Conner Pool

The Chapter 13 plan is a document prepared by your attorney and filed with the court that outlines how you will repay your debts over the life of your plan. In other words, it is a repayment plan. The Chapter 13 plan directs the trustee on how your Chapter 13 payments are to be disbursed to the creditors each month and how long you will be in the plan. A Chapter 13 plan may look different from one district to another, but the essential premise of the document is the same.

What information will be in my plan?

Your plan will at the very least reflect the following:

1. The amount of your Chapter 13 payment and the frequency of how you will pay them (i.e., monthly, biweekly, etc.)

2. The length of time of your plan (anywhere between 36 to 60 months). NOTE: Whether you can have a plan shorter than 60 months will be determined by your household income and/or how much you are paying back to your unsecured creditors.

3. The amount of administrative fees to be paid (i.e., remaining filing fees, attorney fees)

4. How the following debts will be paid in your plan:

   - 100% of priority debts will be paid through the plan (i.e., alimony, child support, and some taxes)
   - How secured debts will be paid through the plan (i.e., automobiles and furniture)
   - How much mortgage arrears will be paid through the plan (if you are keeping your home)
   - What property, if any, you plan on surrendering back to a creditor
   - What executory contracts will be assumed or rejected (i.e., lease, cell phone)
   - What payments you intend to pay directly or that will survive your bankruptcy (i.e., student loans)
   - How much, if any, you will be paying to your unsecured creditors

How will I know how to prepare my plan?

When you file your case, your Bond & Botes attorney will assist you in developing a plan that will work for you. As your case progresses, your Bond & Botes attorney will keep you informed of any changes that may need to be made to your plan after you file your case. The ultimate goal is to have your Chapter 13 plan "confirmed" or approved by the court so that you may continue to make your Chapter 13 payments and be protected from your creditors.

When will my Chapter 13 plan be filed?

Your Chapter 13 plan must be filed within 15 days of your case being filed, but at a Bond & Botes office it will usually be filed on the same day as when your case is filed. As proof of claims come into your case, your Chapter 13 plan may have to be amended to address any debts you forgot to list or correct the amount of debt listed if there is a significant change, but your Bond & Botes attorney will always keep you informed of any necessary changes.

L. What Is the Best Interest in Bankruptcy?

What Is the Best Interest in Bankruptcy?
By Attorney Cynthia T. Lawson

Best interest is one of the factors that must be met in order to have a Chapter 13 plan confirmed or approved by the bankruptcy judge. Best interest tests or liquidation tests are found at 11 U.S.C. §1325(a)(4). This section of the Bankruptcy Code provides that for a Chapter 13 plan to be confirmed, the debtor must be paying to allowed unsecured creditors not less than the amount that would be paid on such claims if the debtor had filed a Chapter 7 bankruptcy. In a nutshell, are creditors in a Chapter 13 getting as much as they would have received in a Chapter 7?

Many times an individual cannot file a Chapter 7 bankruptcy because they have equity in an asset that cannot be protected or exempt. If the individual filed a Chapter 7, the trustee in bankruptcy would sell the asset to pay creditors. If the individual filing bankruptcy does not want to lose the asset, such as a home or vehicle, then sometimes the individual can propose to pay the amount the Chapter 7 trustee would have received from selling the asset to his unsecured creditors in a Chapter 13 in order to keep the asset. In a Chapter 13 the individual has as much as five years to pay that amount to their creditors. The comparison between what the debtor is proposing to pay in the Chapter 13 and the amount the Chapter 7 trustee would have been able to hypothetically pay creditors in a Chapter 7 is the best interest or liquidity test.

Be sure when you meet with an attorney at Bond & Botes you have a good idea of what you owe on loans such as houses or vehicles and an idea of what the asset is worth. Bankruptcy attorneys are not trying to be nosy or intrusive when we ask you for that information. We are simply trying to analyze whether you would lose the asset if you filed a Chapter 7 or whether you would be better off filing a Chapter 13.

M. Can I File Bankruptcy If I Am Unemployed?

Can I File Bankruptcy If I Am Unemployed?
By Attorney Joshua Lawhorn

The short answer is yes. While your monthly income may have an effect on what type of bankruptcy case you file, unemployment itself will usually not prevent you from doing so.

If you seek relief under Chapter 7, not having income from employment could actually work in your favor. The court will determine your average income, and as long as you qualify under the means test, you will be eligible to file. While the means test is somewhat detailed, it basically boils down to whether your household income is more or less than the median for the applicable household size in your state. If it is less, then you should qualify for Chapter 7 relief.

If you seek relief through a Chapter 13 personal reorganization, your monthly income will be more of a factor in getting your case confirmed. In order for your case to be approved by the court, you must be able to show the court that your household income can support the plan payments. The good thing is that it can come from employment, self-employment, social security income, retirement, or even unemployment compensation. As long as you can show to the court that you can support the plan and provide for your monthly living expenses, your case can be confirmed.

There are many factors that go into filing under Chapter 7 and filing a Chapter 13 personal reorganization. That is why it is essential that you are represented by an experienced bankruptcy attorney.

N. Are Co-Debtors Protected If I File for Bankruptcy?

Are Co-Debtors Protected If I File for Bankruptcy?
By Attorney Joshua C. Lawhorn

When someone incurs debt, it is very common to have a co-signor, or co-debtor, on that loan. If the person paying the loan defaults, the creditor can seek the balance from the primary debtor or the co-debtor. If one co-debtor seeks debt relief in bankruptcy, what happens to the other debtor? The answer primarily depends on the type of case the debtor filed. In general, if someone files for Chapter 7 bankruptcy, the co-debtor is not protected. The filer's dischargeable debts are wiped out and they are no longer liable for those debts. The creditor will be able to collect from the non-filing co-debtor. However, if that person files for Chapter 13 relief, the protection of the automatic stay is extended to the co-debtor for most debts. If it is a consumer debt, the co-debtor is protected for at least as long as the primary debtor stays in the plan. Completion of the plan will usually absolve both the debtor and the co-debtor of the debt if the debt was paid through the plan. Again, Chapter 13 co-debtor protection applies to consumer debts. The question of when a co-debtor is protected is one that should be addressed in a consultation with an experienced attorney. It should also be noted that if a person seeks debt relief, it does not leave the co-debtor without options. For example, if two people co-sign on an automobile, the payments are current, and one of the debtors files for bankruptcy, the non-filer can usually continue to make payments and keep the vehicle. By abandoning the vehicle to the co-debtor, it allows the co-debtor to maintain payments as if the case was never filed. This is, of course, just one possibility that can be addressed when you meet with an attorney. There are many possibilities when a person seeks debt relief, and these sometimes affect other people. There is no person to better assist you getting the best relief possible than an experienced bankruptcy attorney.

O. Can a School Withhold My Transcripts If I Included My School Tuition in My Bankruptcy?

Can a School Withhold My Transcripts If I Included My School Tuition in My Bankruptcy? By Attorney Mary Conner Pool

NO, not if you filed in the Middle District of Alabama. On March 18, 2013, the Honorable Dwight H. Williams, Jr. held that Troy University willfully violated the automatic stay in a Chapter 13 when they refused to release an official transcript to the debtor since she filed bankruptcy. 11 U.S.C. § 362(a)(6) prevents an entity from performing "any act to collect, assess, or recover a claim against the debtor that arose before the commencement of the case." Troy University was found to have knowledge of the bankruptcy and the automatic stay when it refused to release the debtor's transcripts. Judge Williams held that Troy violated the automatic stay because the only motive for Troy to withhold the transcript was to get the debtor to pay her pre-petition tuition.

Judge Williams held that a school could charge customary or requisite fees that are necessary to produce or create official transcripts.

Most bankruptcy courts nationwide have the same rules regarding transcripts, and the case law about this is fairly universal. It is important to ask your local counsel about this issue.

P. What Is a 341 Meeting of Creditors?

What Is a 341 Meeting of Creditors?
By Attorney Amy K. Tanner

A meeting of creditors is a mandatory hearing that is held approximately 30 days after the filing of any consumer bankruptcy case. It is commonly referred to as the §341 meeting of creditors as this is the code section found in Title 11 of the United States Bankruptcy Code, which mandates or requires this hearing be held. It is normally presided over by the United States trustee or a representative of the trustee. The court, i.e., judge, may not conduct or attend this meeting.

Who must attend this meeting? It is mandatory for all debtors and debtors' attorneys to attend a meeting of creditors. Each debtor is required to take an oath in which they swear or affirm that they will tell the truth. The creditors that each debtor has listed are also invited to attend this meeting, but there is no requirement that they attend. However, they may come to the meeting to ask the debtor questions about the debt they have with that particular creditor. The most common creditors in attendance at these meetings are automobile lien holders, who usually want to verify that their collateral is insured. Most creditors are courteous to the debtors at these meetings; it is generally not a scary "grilling" session.

The trustee, or representative of the trustee, who presides over the meeting of creditors may ask the debtor questions about the petition and schedules that the debtor has filed with the court. The Chapter 13 meeting of creditors also serves as a good forum to address or point out any minor issues or changes that need to be made to the debtor's plan in order to get the plan ready for confirmation. At the Chapter 7 meeting of creditors, the trustee is required to examine the debtor to determine that they are aware of the consequences of receiving a discharge in bankruptcy, the opportunity to have filed other chapters of bankruptcy in order to repay creditors, the effects of receiving a discharge, and the effects of reaffirming any debts. These meetings are normally brief, efficient, and quite painless for the debtors.

Q. Will I Continue to Pay Interest to My Creditors That I Include in My Chapter 13 Bankruptcy?

Will I Continue to Pay Interest to Creditors Included in My Chapter 13 Bankruptcy?
By Attorney Amy Tanner

For most people who file a Chapter 13 or debt consolidation bankruptcy, one of the huge benefits is the ability to discharge certain interest and penalties on certain debts. In just about all Chapter 13 cases, particularly those filed by debtors who are below the state median income, interest on all unsecured debt is dischargeable. This can be a huge savings for a debtor, particularly if one is struggling with the high interest rates of credit cards and payday loans. It can definitely give some light at the end of the tunnel as far as getting these debts taken care of in a reasonable time. In some cases, if you are an above-median-income debtor, the court may require you to pay a small percentage of interest on your unsecured debt. This is still a great savings from contract or judgment rates of interest, usually no more than a few percent.

For most secured debts paid through a Chapter 13, you are required to pay interest at the current Chapter 13 plan rate. This rate will vary across the federal court districts but is loosely determined by the current prime rate plus a few points for various risk factors. However, the plan rate is almost always substantially lower than the contract rate of interest.

A Chapter 13 debtor is also eligible to discharge future interest and penalty on most federal tax debt and state tax debt. In many circumstances, tax debt is not dischargeable in bankruptcy; however, by including your tax debt in a Chapter 13 payment plan, a debtor can reap the benefit of discharging future interest and penalties that would accrue outside of a Chapter 13 plan. This applies to taxes that have come due prior to the filing of a Chapter 13 case. This benefit can be very helpful to someone who may be facing tax debt where it would be difficult to pay the amount owed along with the added interest and penalty that would normally accrue.

R. How Long Can I Stay in My House If I Am Giving It up in Bankruptcy?

How Long Can I Stay in My House If
I Am Giving It up in Bankruptcy?
By Attorney Ronald C. Sykstus

Many of our clients have this particular question with regard to bankruptcy if they are giving up or "surrendering" their house in bankruptcy. Our advice to clients is to stay in the house until the foreclosure sale date. As a general rule, it takes quite a while for most mortgage companies to foreclose on a home. As a result, if our clients move out prior to the foreclosure, then they still may be responsible for utilities, insurance, and any city or municipal requirements such as lawn care and maintenance. Because of that, the most prudent solution is for clients to stay in the house until the foreclosure sale date, which actually is the mechanism by which mortgage companies transfer properties back to themselves. Several bankruptcy courts have held that there is no discharge injunction violation if a mortgage company refuses to either foreclose on a property or release a lien on a residence. If a mortgage company refuses to or fails to foreclose on a home, then, as a general rule, the buyer of the property will remain responsible for the payment of taxes, insurance, and maintenance. What that allows for, then, is essentially a free pass to allow people to live in a property without a mortgage payment and to simply keep up the taxes, insurance, and maintenance on the property. This is the best course of action for anyone considering filing either a Chapter 7 or Chapter 13 bankruptcy and giving up or "surrendering" their interest in a home.

Our advice is to save the money you would use to pay the mortgage principal and interest and put it aside for moving costs and a down payment for your new place if and when the mortgage company finally forecloses. Every situation is different and the facts of every situation should be discussed in detail with an experienced attorney.

S. If I Am Surrendering My House in Bankruptcy, How Should I Go About It?

If I Am Surrendering My House in Bankruptcy, How Should I Go About It? By Attorney Ronald C. Sykstus

If you are giving up or "surrendering" your house in bankruptcy, our initial advice to our clients, as discussed, is to stay in the house until the foreclosure sale date for the reasons set forth above. As a general rule, it takes quite a while for most mortgage companies to foreclose on a home if and when the mortgage company finally forecloses. **Again, please keep the property maintained and cared for as far as any homeowner's association requirements, utilities, lawn and shrubbery, etc., UNTIL the actual foreclosure sale by the mortgage company when a foreclosure deed is filed with the probate court.**

Once you are all set to leave your house, make sure you have removed everything. Clean the house and leave it in a broom-swept condition. Once you "officially" leave the house, you will not be able to return. Once you have moved everything out, write a letter to each mortgage holder (first, second, and third mortgage companies, if any), enclose a key to the home, and give them this information in the letter you prepare:

(Use this as a sample only and create your own actual letter)

Date
Mortgage Company Name
Full mailing address of mortgage company
Re: Your full name, address of home, BK case #

Dear Sir/Ma'am:

As you are aware, we have filed bankruptcy on our home located at (full address of home). Our bankruptcy case number is (list #) and it was filed in the State of (name of state you filed in). We have officially moved out of the house. As a result, we wanted to give you notice of our official departure and let you know that you can secure the house as soon as possible. To allow you access to the house, we have enclosed a key with this letter.

Thank you for your immediate attention to this matter. Also, because of the bankruptcy filing, please ensure that we are not contacted by your company by phone or in writing ever again. Thank you.

Your full name(s) printed and signed

Your full mailing address

Please ensure you keep a copy of the signed letter you send and also please be sure to mail it by certified mail, return receipt requested. Please also always keep the returned green card of receipt so that you can prove, if necessary, that you notified the mortgage company or companies, if more than one, of your departure.

T. How Soon After Chapter 7 Bankruptcy Can You Buy a New House?

How Soon After Chapter 7 Bankruptcy Can You Buy a New House? By Attorney Bradford W. Botes

A common bankruptcy myth is that it takes seven years after filing bankruptcy before you can get new credit. This is simply untrue. Any kind of bankruptcy can be reported on your credit for up to ten years, but this does not mean that you can't obtain new credit during the ten-year period. In fact, most of our clients receive letters shortly after they receive their bankruptcy discharge with offers of new credit. Many automobile dealerships advertise that they will finance a car purchase following a bankruptcy discharge.

Why is this? The truth is that someone who files bankruptcy is usually much less of a credit risk after filing bankruptcy than they were before having done so. Prior to filing bankruptcy, the individual had multiple creditors. A new lender that made a loan to the individual would have to compete with other creditors in order to be paid. The new lender would also need to be concerned with a bankruptcy being filed in the near future, thereby discharging all of the debt owed. Following bankruptcy, the individual is often debt-free. Therefore, the new lender will not have to compete with other creditors in order to be paid. Further, if the individual filed a Chapter 7 bankruptcy, she will not be able to do so again for another eight years. Thus the new lender will have little worry about his debt being discharged in a future bankruptcy.

But what about buying a house? How soon after filing a Chapter 7 bankruptcy can you buy a new house? Our experience has been that it takes two years after your discharge in order to get a decent mortgage. You may be able to get a mortgage sooner, but your interest rate will not be as low as it would be if you waited two years. This is important because you will be making payments that include the higher interest rate for as long as 30 years. You can save a good bit of money if you can wait long enough after the discharge to obtain a lower interest rate.

In addition to the above information, much will depend on how you manage your finances following your bankruptcy. If you keep a particular debt (often done through a reaffirmation agreement during the bankruptcy) like a house or car payment, be certain to make the payment on a timely basis following the bankruptcy. Try to save some money so that you will be able to make a down payment. In short, your actions following the bankruptcy will have a significant bearing on your ability to buy a home.

U. How Long Can I Keep My Car After Filing Chapter 7 Straight Bankruptcy?

How Long Can I Keep My Car After Filing
Chapter 7 Straight Bankruptcy?
By Attorney Bradford W. Botes

Chapter 7 bankruptcy, often referred to as "straight bankruptcy," is a proceeding through which an honest debtor can discharge most if not all of her debt. Although technically the Bankruptcy Code allows a trustee to liquidate (sell) some of the debtor's assets and divide the proceeds amongst his creditors, in reality this very seldom happens. In the vast majority of Chapter 7 bankruptcies, the debtor is able to exempt the assets which he owns and thereby prevent the trustee from selling them. We refer to this as a "no asset bankruptcy."

Although a debtor can discharge debt in a Chapter 7 bankruptcy, sometimes difficult decisions need to be made when it comes to a secured creditor. A secured creditor is a creditor that has a lien against property owned by the debtor. For instance, when you borrow money to buy a car, the lender normally places a lien on the car's title. Upon filing Chapter 7 bankruptcy, the debtor must express her intentions with respect to the secured creditor. Generally, the debtor can either surrender the car and discharge the debt, agree to keep paying for the car (reaffirm the debt), or pay the creditor the value of the car in a lump sum (redeem the collateral).

Keeping Your Car

So how long can the debtor keep his/her car after filing Chapter 7 bankruptcy if he/she doesn't want to keep paying for it and can't afford to pay the creditor the car's value in a lump sum? Must the car be surrendered immediately? The answer is no. In many cases, our clients retain their cars for weeks if not months after filing bankruptcy. This is true because the creditor cannot simply come and get the car after the bankruptcy is filed. Upon filing, the bankruptcy court issues an order called an automatic stay, which prohibits creditors from collecting money owed by the debtor. The creditor must either seek the court's permission to gain possession of the car (seek relief from the automatic stay) or wait until the bankruptcy process is over. Since many car lenders will finance a new car for an honest debtor immediately after their bankruptcy discharge, debtors often go no time at all between surrendering the old car and buying a new one.

Please note that in order to retain the options set forth above, the debtor must still have possession of the car when his Chapter 7 bankruptcy is filed. If the car is repossessed prior to filing, these options may not exist. It is therefore important to seek the advice of experienced bankruptcy counsel before you get too far into debt. Don't wait until it is too late to explore your options.

V. What Is a Reaffirmation Agreement in Bankruptcy?

What Is a Reaffirmation Agreement in Bankruptcy?
By Attorney Amy K. Tanner

Simply stated, a reaffirmation agreement is an agreement that a debtor in a Chapter 7 bankruptcy enters into with a creditor that reaffirms or re-obligates the terms of the original contract with that creditor. Reaffirmation agreements are applicable in Chapter 7 bankruptcy. If there is no undue hardship to you, you may have a creditor that you want to continue to pay after filing a Chapter 7 (straight) bankruptcy. These agreements are usually utilized when a debtor wants to keep a vehicle or a home.

When you file your Chapter 7 petition with the bankruptcy court, you will also file a statement of intentions. This is usually where you state your desire to reaffirm with a particular secured creditor. It is very helpful to be contractually current on the debt that you wish to reaffirm and to have the collateral (i.e., home or auto) properly insured. It is generally not advised to reaffirm a debt with an unsecured creditor. It is important, however, that you discuss your personal desires about maintaining a relationship with a particular creditor with your attorney to determine if you might be putting yourself in a position of undue hardship.

If you have expressed your desire to reaffirm a debt, the creditor will, in most circumstances, provide you and your attorney with a reaffirmation agreement that must be signed by you, your attorney, and the creditor and then filed with the bankruptcy court in order to be enforceable.

We strongly advise all of our clients to seriously consider the financial commitment you are making when entering into a reaffirmation agreement with any creditor to insure that you are not putting yourself in a hardship situation.

W. How Soon After Chapter 7 Bankruptcy Can You Buy a New Car?

How Soon After Chapter 7 Bankruptcy Can You Buy a New Car?
By Attorney Bradford W. Botes

The answer is immediately—really. Virtually every person who comes to one of our offices seeking assistance with their financial problems is concerned with the impact that a bankruptcy filing will have on their credit. This is, of course, a valid concern. People we assist have often been dealing with collectors and credit issues for quite some time. They have put off coming to see us because of their concern about the impact that a bankruptcy filing will have on their credit.

As I have written previously, filing bankruptcy is often the first step that one can take to rebuild credit. Prior to filing a Chapter 7 bankruptcy, you are awash with debt and, from the perspective of a prospective creditor, a candidate for bankruptcy. Upon receiving your bankruptcy discharge, you are debt-free and unable to seek Chapter 7 bankruptcy protection again for another eight years. Looked upon in this manner, you are much less of a credit risk following your bankruptcy discharge.

This is why you will find that many if not most car dealerships advertise that they can provide financing for the purchase of a new or used vehicle immediately after you receive your bankruptcy discharge. If you have difficulty believing this, take a look at this Sunday's newspaper and look at the automobile ads. Or call a car dealer and ask to speak to the finance manager. Assuming that you have steady employment and an income to support a car payment, you will most often find financing available.

X. How Will Filing for Bankruptcy Affect My Government Security Clearance?

How Will Filing for Bankruptcy Affect My Government Security Clearance?
By Attorney Ronald C. Sykstus

Many of our clients are active duty military or government employees or employees who work for defense contractors. As a result, many of these prospective clients will have either secret or top secret security clearances, which are required for their jobs. A common question we are asked is "How will filing for bankruptcy affect my security clearance?" DOD (Department of Defense) Directive 5220.6 covers all matters regarding security clearances for the government. For clients who have debts and debt problems, Guideline F is the applicable provision regarding financial affairs to determine whether there will be a potential problem. Paragraph 20 of Guideline F in the DOD Directive sets forth circumstances that mitigate security concerns. Paragraph 20(d) states that "the individual initiated a good-faith effort to repay creditors or otherwise resolve debts." That paragraph covers the filing of either a Chapter 7 or a Chapter 13 bankruptcy. Additionally, Paragraph 20(b) of the Directive can be used to explain how a person got into a financial fix prior to the bankruptcy having been filed. As a general proposition, and in our experience, we have seen that one bankruptcy in a lifetime will not cause any security clearance issues. If, however, there are other issues, then that could be problematic. For instance, we have seen situations where two bankruptcy filings fifteen years apart were enough to revoke a clearance. Additionally, a bankruptcy filing with a criminal conviction (DUI, domestic abuse, etc.) may also cause a clearance to be revoked. The government usually tries to add a charge to any security case under Guideline E, which deals with personal conduct. The easiest way for this charge to be alleged under Guideline E is for lack of candor in the applicant's answer to the SF86 Form, which is the government form completed under oath in order to get a clearance. It covers an individual's entire background, including financial history. With regard to the financial questions, applicants are asked if they have ever been sued, if they have ever had a judgment against them, if they have ever been delinquent more than 60 days, 90 days, and 120 days with any debts, etc. With those types of questions, applicants invariably and mistakenly get tripped up, and an incorrect answer can be used against them.

In most circumstances, filing for bankruptcy should not be a security problem to address debts if finances have not been a recurrent, lifelong problem. Prior to submitting an initial security clearance application, or in anticipation of a renewal for a clearance, we always advise clients to get their free credit reports from www.annualcreditreport.com. Review the credit reports and see exactly what is out there. If there are delinquent debts, please seek advice on how to address them. Our website discusses in more detail the actual security clearance application process. Additionally, our website also sets forth exactly how you can get your true, free credit reports from www.annualcreditreport.com. Finally, if you do have a security clearance and you file for bankruptcy, we advise you to notify your facility security officer (FSO) of the bankruptcy filing. In most circumstances, the FSO will simply want a copy of the petition. Again, complete candor in all matters dealing with your security clearance is the absolute best way to protect your clearance.

Y. Payday Advance Issues and Bankruptcy

Can I Include Payday Loans in a Bankruptcy?
By Attorney Grant McNutt

This is a question that I am asked quite often, and the simple answer is yes! Unfortunately, many people get involved with payday lenders just trying to make ends meet. They then get into a vicious cycle of paying exorbitant interest on a post-dated check every week out of fear that the payday lender will present the check to their bank and that it will bounce, i.e., be returned as non-sufficient funds.

Once a client has decided that bankruptcy is a viable option, our advice regarding payday lenders who are holding previously written checks is to go immediately to their bank and stop payment on those checks or, if our client has authorized an automatic debit, to stop payment on that as well. We further advise our clients that, out of an abundance of caution, it is best to go ahead and close that bank account to avoid any electronic transactions that the payday lender may attempt, but only after implementing the stop payments on checks or automatic transactions.

This method has proven to be the safest way to avoid a non-sufficient funds check or presentation of a check on a closed account, as these are matters that can be turned over to the district attorney for criminal prosecution and collection. Therefore, it is imperative that you stop payment on the check and/or automatic debit AND close the account they are associated with—exactly in that order.

What if a client has already had a check from a payday lender returned for non-sufficient funds? In the majority of cases, and from our experience here in Alabama, most payday lenders and cash advance lenders are very cooperative with the bankruptcy process and rarely will turn over non-sufficient funds instrument to the district attorney for prosecution. Further, here in Alabama, the district attorneys have not made it a practice to collect for the payday lenders.

If you are caught up in this payday loan cycle and feel that you may need bankruptcy assistance to help you, please contact one of our offices nearest to you. Set up a free consultation to speak with one of our licensed attorneys, who can further advise you about this matter and any other financial problems that you are experiencing.

Can I Be Arrested for Defaulting on My Payday Loan?
By Attorney Amy K. Tanner

The short answer to this question is no! This question usually comes to me or my colleagues from a frightened victim of this "payday loan scam" after they have been contacted by a self-labeled "collector" plying intimidating scare tactics to collect on a debt. Many times the victim does not even owe these so-called "collectors," and it is just a scammer who has obtained the victim's information via public records. These scammers then try to intimidate the victim into paying some money on the spot.

The first and foremost, best advice that I can give a potential victim is to **NOT** give the caller any personal information at all, to include bank account numbers, debit card numbers, or social security numbers. The normal scenario is that a person will receive a telephone call from someone claiming to be a federal officer. This person tells the victim that there is a warrant for their arrest for default on a payday loan. The caller will then offer the victim an "opportunity" to get out of the warrant by paying the debt over the phone by debit card. Sometimes, they will threaten to come to your place of employment the next day and arrest you. I have heard of some who actually threaten bodily harm. If you receive or have received threats of this nature and fear for your safety, contact local law enforcement immediately.

Of course, these types of collection efforts are in clear violation of the Federal Debt Collections Practices Act (FDCPA); however, the overwhelming majority of these calls come from offshore call centers, making it impossible to prosecute them. Many of these calls are "ghosted" through a U.S. telephone number, making them seem more real. The caller will never comply with a request to provide proof of the debt in writing.

In brief, short of proving that a victim has committed fraud, a collector or payday loan company cannot arrest you for defaulting on your payday loan. The only entity who can bring any criminal charges against you is the district attorney of the county that you live in.

The Payday Loan Treadmill
By Attorney Bradford W. Botes

In recent years, many areas have seen a proliferation of title and payday loan stores. These businesses typically make small short-term loans to consumers who don't think other options exist. The stores are everywhere and the loans are easy to make. Please be cautious: Repayment of the loans can be very difficult and anything but short term.

Recently, I met with a nice retired older lady who had taken a payday loan from a well-known title loan company. She borrowed $2,200 in early 2009 and made monthly payments of $248 until December of 2012. At that time, the lender "lowered" her interest rate and her payments dropped to $109 per month. As of today, the balance on the loan has not decreased. It is still the original $2,200. By my calculations she has paid in excess of $10,000 toward a $2,200 loan.

In my experience, the story above is not unusual. Desperate people start with just one payday loan that they are certain can be paid off the next month. Next month comes and they struggle simply to make the interest payment and renew the loan for another month. Often, they borrow from one payday lender to pay what is owed to another. I call this the "The Payday Loan Treadmill." If only the interest is paid, the cash-strapped consumer simply goes another month without making any progress in paying down the loan's balance. When another urgent need for cash develops, the consumer may go to another payday lender in order to have enough to pay the interest on the first and enough left over to address the current need. By the next month, there are two interest payments to be made. It is as if someone has turned up the speed on the treadmill. The consumer is working harder and harder yet making no progress. The anxiety caused by the ongoing debt cycle can be overwhelming.

From a collective perspective, there is clearly a need for legislation to curb the practices of short-term, high-interest loan businesses. That will be the topic of another blog post. The purpose of this post is to encourage people to avoid high-interest, short-term loans. Seek other alternatives. Once you get on the payday loan treadmill, it may be difficult to get off.

If you do find yourself overwhelmed by this or any other type of debt, you should consult with an experienced and qualified professional before things get worse. Options are available.

Z. Can You File Bankruptcy on a Timeshare?

Can You File Bankruptcy on a Timeshare?
By Attorney Amy K. Tanner

Getting twisted into a timeshare can be a real life lesson. Sometimes that is what will drive people to look at bankruptcy in the first place. The simple answer as to whether or not you can file bankruptcy on a timeshare is yes. There are, however, some intricacies in including a timeshare in a bankruptcy. The Bankruptcy Abuse Prevention and Consumer Protection Act (BAPCPA) enacted in 2005 made a multitude of changes to the law governing bankruptcy, and it specifically addresses timeshares. The majority of folks want to get rid of or get out from under the obligation of a timeshare by including it in their bankruptcy. You can surrender a time share in either a Chapter 13 or Chapter 7 bankruptcy.

The best way to do this is reject it as an executory contract. The nuance here is that any maintenance fees that come due post-bankruptcy filing will continue to accrue against a debtor, and the majority opinion based on BAPCPA is that they are non-dischargeable. Therefore, what we advise most of our clients to do is to immediately get in touch with the timeshare company and deed the property back to them to avoid accrual of non-dischargeable post-bankruptcy fees on the timeshare.

There are a few people who may be completely up to date with all timeshare expenses and wish to retain the timeshare instead of including it in bankruptcy. Whether or not this is feasible will probably depend on where you live and what district you are filing your bankruptcy case. Therefore, it is good to get advice from competent legal counsel in your area. As an aside, if you are thinking of ever buying a timeshare, based upon what we have seen, please don't! You will save yourself a lifetime of headaches! In the end, it is very difficult and cumbersome to try and shed yourself of a timeshare, especially in light of the fact that no one will want to buy it from you.

Chapter 13

What Should I do If I Am Sued? How to Defend a Lawsuit and the Potential Consequences If You Do Not

Oftentimes, clients will come to us after they have been sued by a creditor or debt collector. In some situations, clients will have waited until after the lawsuit has been filed and a judgment has been entered against them. It is our considered professional opinion that any time someone receives a lawsuit, they should talk with a lawyer immediately. Waiting will not make the situation any better, and it will most definitely make it worse. Once a lawsuit is filed against someone, there can be dramatic and long-term negative consequences on several fronts. We cannot overstate the importance of talking to an attorney and defending yourself on a lawsuit immediately upon receipt. The long-term ramifications are critical—from credit report nightmares to loss of substantial property, including homes, to garnishment of wages and seizures of bank accounts and other property—and counsel in this type of situation cannot be understated.

What Can I Do If I Am Being Sued by a Creditor or Debt Collector?
By Attorney Ronald C. Sykstus

If you receive a summons stating that you have been sued by a debt collector or creditor, do not ignore it! You have a right to request a trial and to demand that the plaintiff (the entity bringing the lawsuit) prove its case in court. If you do not timely file an answer to a lawsuit, then you will automatically lose under what is called a default judgment. The plaintiff will then be able to proceed with collections against you on the default judgment that it received. You must file an answer on time with the court where the lawsuit is pending and also mail a copy of your answer to the plaintiff. Failure to timely file an answer with the court will result in a default judgment against you! Below is a sample of what an answer should look like. If your answer is anything other than a denial of the complaint, you will lose automatically.

It is our advice to deny the allegations in order to force the plaintiff to rightfully prove its case. You also have the right to assert affirmative defenses such as statute of limitations, etc. Additionally, many times a debt collector has somehow decided it can pursue you on an old debt but will be unable to prove it in court due to an inability to comply with the rules of evidence. The sample answer below is only a sample; every individual case is different based upon its unique facts. If you have other debts that you are behind on, it may make sense to at least explore how a bankruptcy option may help you. If you have no other debts, or if all of your debts are current and this pending lawsuit is the only issue you face, it may make sense just to defend on the lawsuit itself. Our attorneys can assist with either a bankruptcy option or just a defense to the lawsuit. Either way, please pay immediate attention to the lawsuit and do not miss the time to answer it.

*****The following is a sample answer only and is not meant to be construed as legal advice but is only to be used for general information. Each case should be discussed with an attorney first since every case and fact situation is different.** ***

IN THE (Type in name of court) **COURT OF** (Type in name of county) **COUNTY,** (Type in name of state) **STATE**

x (Type in the plaintiff's name),

Plaintiff(s),

vs. **CIVIL ACTION NO.:**(Put the exact case number that is on the lawsuit here)

x (Type in defendant's name),
x (Type in additional defendants' names),

(List the name of each and every defendant)

Defendant(s).

ANSWER TO COMPLAINT

NOW COMES the Defendant(s), and hereby denies all of the allegations contained in the Complaint.

The Defendant(s) respectfully requests a trial in this case.

Respectfully Submitted,

(Print your full name and mailing address and sign)
Defendant 1

(Print your full name and mailing address and sign)
Defendant 2

CERTIFICATE OF SERVICE

I have filed a copy of this Answer with the county_____ court on the _____ day of _____, (year) and I have also mailed a copy to the Plaintiff on the _____ day of _____, (year).

(Defendant's signature)________________________
Defendant 1

(Defendant's signature)________________________
Defendant 2

What Can I Do If I Am Sued for a Debt in Justice Court in Mississippi?
By Attorney Ed Woods

In Mississippi, each county has a justice court. These courts are staffed by not less than two or more than five part-time judges and other staff. Justice courts hear small civil, i.e., non-criminal, claims and misdemeanor criminal cases. A "small" civil claim is defined as a claim of $3,500 or less, excluding court filing fees, which usually run between $64 and $74. A justice court cannot hear a civil case where more than $3,500 is being demanded. Debt collectors frequently use justice court to collect their small claims because cases proceed much faster in justice court than other courts, and there are other advantages as well. If you are sued in justice court for a debt, don't panic and don't ignore it. Following are ten tips to help you deal with the experience.

1. You need not hire an attorney to represent you. However, as with all legal matters, the best practice is to seek the assistance of a competent attorney when confronted with any legal matter. You will not receive any favorable treatment because you are representing yourself.

2. Don't ignore the matter. Attend the hearing scheduled in your case. If you fail to attend your hearing, the party suing you wins by "default." There is a special rule in justice court that requires the court to enter judgment against you if you fail to attend your hearing after receiving notice of the hearing date. The judge has no choice under these circumstances.

3. Dress appropriately for your hearing. You want to be taken seriously, and your attire should reflect this desire. It is very difficult to command respect in jeans and a T-shirt.

4. The party suing you has the burden of proving their claim against you. You have the right to ask that party to produce the evidence necessary to do this. In debt cases, this means the party should produce a copy of the promissory note or other proper evidence to prove that: (a) you owe the claimed debt in the first place, and (b) the amount sued for is the correct balance on the debt. If the party suing you cannot produce proper supporting documentation, you should ask the judge to dismiss the lawsuit "with prejudice." This means that the party cannot re-file the case against you at a later date.

5. Just like the party suing you must produce proper evidence to support their claim, you must produce proper evidence supporting your defense of the claim. For example, if you admit that you owe the debt but you disagree with the amount being demanded, you should have payment receipts with you at your hearing and be prepared to show and explain the correct balance on the debt. If there is a witness who can help you establish your defense, that witness must appear in court to give live testimony. A note or letter from a witness cannot be considered by the court.

6. Always, always, always show the utmost respect for the judge, court personnel, all witnesses, the opposing party, and any attorneys appearing in the case. In the event that any of these persons treats you rudely or disrespectfully, maintain your composure and treat them with respect. Never lose your temper with anyone regardless of how they treat you.

7. When it is your turn to testify, always address your testimony to the judge by looking and speaking directly to him or her. Never argue with the opposing party or that party's attorney. You have the right to

ask questions of the opposing party and any witnesses called by the opposing party. Keep your questions direct and relevant to the claims and defenses being considered. Don't ask questions just for the sake of asking. This tactic really irritates judges. If you have no relevant questions, politely tell the court you have no questions of this witness.

8. Unless you are sitting while testifying from the witness stand, you should stand up when speaking to the court. If there is a podium in the courtroom, stand at the podium to address the court.

9. Just like the oath says, you must tell the truth, the whole truth, and nothing but the truth. If there are certain true facts which are not favorable to you, be prepared to freely admit these facts to the court. Never try to con a judge. Judges are particularly adept at detecting when a witness is being less than truthful about something. Such a tactic will destroy your credibility with the judge and will likely severely damage your case.

10. If the party suing you asks the court for a continuance of the case, tell the court that you do not agree to any further delays. Often, debt collectors come to court minimally prepared or not prepared at all. They assume that you will not contest their lawsuit and that they will win by default. When the collector sees you in court and prepared to defend yourself, they ask for more time to get prepared. Don't let them get away with this tactic. Politely and firmly tell the court that you are present and ready to proceed now. Politely remind the court that the collector is the party who brought the suit in the first place. They have had ample time to prepare.

If the worst happens and you do have a judgment entered against you, you have 30 days to appeal. Depending on the specifics of your case, it may be a waste of time and money to appeal. A proper decision about a possible appeal is best made with the advice of a competent attorney. Our firm has caring and experienced attorneys who have helped people solve their financial problems for many years. If you are experiencing money problems, we can help. We meet with clients in the Jackson, Hattiesburg, Vicksburg, and Gulf Coast areas in Mississippi. Your first visit with our firm is free of charge. At this visit, we will discuss your situation and identify your options. Often, a consolidation of all of your debts under Chapter 13 is the best option. You can consolidate mortgage payments, car payments, finance company loans, past due taxes, student loans, payday and check cashing loans, credit cards, medical bills, and all your other debts into one affordable monthly payment. You are protected from your creditors while you are making these payments. At the end of a three- or five-year period, you are finished and any amounts you weren't able to pay are discharged; you will never have to pay these amounts. In some cases, filing a Chapter 7 straight bankruptcy case may be the best option. This would allow you to eliminate certain types of debt entirely if you qualify. The important thing to remember is that you have choices. We're here to help you make the right choice for you.

If you do not fight a lawsuit and you lose, then the dramatic post-judgment collection actions can begin against you. Two examples are judgment and judicial liens against your property and garnishment of your wages. These two topics are discussed below.

Judgments and Judicial Liens in the State of Alabama
By Attorney Ronald C. Sykstus

In Alabama, if a judgment is entered against you, the creditor who got the judgment can do several things to collect on the judgment. The creditor can garnish wages and bank accounts; it can force the sheriff to seize your home, real estate, and personal property. It can also place a judgment lien on your home (also referred to as a judicial lien) and real estate through the probate office. These judgment liens grow at a rate of 12 percent or more per year and can encumber your home and real estate for up to a ten-year period. The judgment lien can also be renewed for another ten years at the end of the first ten-year period. As a result, this could prohibit a refinance or sale of the real property unless the judgment lien plus interest is paid in full.

If you are sued in the state of Alabama, it is very important to fight any lawsuit at the beginning and to do whatever you can to prevent a judgment from being entered in the first place.

A bankruptcy filing can avoid a judgment lien/judicial lien on your real estate to the extent it impairs your allowed exemptions. As a result, it is of critical importance that you research at the local probate office in the county in which you live, and have lived for at least the last ten years, and in which you have any real estate to see if any judgment lien has been recorded against you. If any such liens exist, please make sure to get a copy of that to your bankruptcy attorney prior to filing your bankruptcy case. We cannot overstate the importance of doing so in order to make sure that you get a true fresh start if you choose to file for bankruptcy relief.

What Is a Judicial Lien and Can I Resolve a Judicial Lien by Filing Bankruptcy?
By Attorney Amy K. Tanner

When you have a debt that has been reduced to a judgment amount within a state court proceeding, that judgment can be filed with the probate court of the county in which you reside. The result of this filing is that it is now a judgment or judicial lien that will attach to any equity in real property you currently own or any real property you may acquire in the future. The ultimate ending is that the debt for this lien must be resolved by payment or some method before you can sell or transfer your currently owned real property or, in most cases, purchase new real property. The creditor holding the judicial lien may also choose to execute on the lien. This means that the creditor would force a legal sale of your real property in order to obtain the amount of the underlying debt or judgment amount.

Most all liens can be avoided within some type of bankruptcy filing. The appropriate United State Code Section that allows the avoidance of judicial liens is 11 U.S.C. Section 522(f) (2) (A), (B), and (C). Upon the filing of any type of bankruptcy, the automatic stay will go into place and stay any execution on the judicial lien.

Whether or not you should file a Chapter 7 straight bankruptcy or a Chapter 13 debt consolidation depends on many factors, to include whether or not you currently own property and have equity in real or personal property. It can further depend on whether or not the real property you own is your homestead, as judicial liens are only avoidable under bankruptcy as applicable to your homestead property.

If you currently own no real property or if you own real property that has no equity in it at the time of filing bankruptcy, and are otherwise eligible, a Chapter 7 bankruptcy may be your best alternative to simply discharge the underlying debt that gave rise to the judicial lien and avoid the lien under Section 522 as referenced above.

If you own real estate, and have any amount of equity in that real estate, it is likely advisable to file a Chapter 13 debt consolidation so that you may pay the debt giving rise to the judicial lien, either in full or in part, and also avoid the lien as to future property interest.

It is imperative that judicial liens be handled under your bankruptcy in a timely manner. It is very important to be aware of any and all judicial liens against you and that you provide that information to your attorney at the outset of your case.

What Are My Options on a Garnishment?
By Attorney Ed Woods

A garnishment is a serious situation. Ignoring a garnishment can hurt you. Generally speaking, a garnishment is a type of legal proceeding that allows someone you owe to seize your non-exempt property to satisfy a debt. In Mississippi, and most states, the usual targets of a garnishment are a percentage of your wages and all of your bank account balances (up to the amount you owe) which may be seized by order of a court for payment on a debt. A common and serious problem with bank account seizures is that such seizures commonly occur with joint accounts. So, if you are a joint account holder with someone else, their money is often taken along with yours to satisfy the debt. Further, current Mississippi law does not limit the type of property that may be subject to garnishment. So, garnishments aren't necessarily limited to wages and bank account balances. Garnishments can wreak havoc on your monthly finances and deprive you of money you need for basic necessities such as food, medicine, clothing, and shelter. Having your wages garnished for more than one single debt may lead to loss of employment.

The good news is that there are effective options available to you. But, you must act quickly. The worst possible thing you can do in the face of a garnishment is to ignore it and procrastinate. Immediately seek legal advice from a competent and experienced debt relief attorney so that your situation can be properly analyzed and appropriate action can be taken. Don't listen to the stories others tell you about how they have handled (or would handle) a garnishment. For some reason, garnishments have a place in the popular imagination and, in over two decades of law practice, I have heard some of the most incredible tales about garnishment situations and how they are resolved. While quite entertaining, these tales are always based on myth and misinformation about this simple, but powerful, way to collect a debt. Below are a few general things to think about if you are facing (or about to face) a garnishment. Again, however, the need for immediate and competent legal advice cannot be overemphasized. Self-help in this situation is dangerous and may make matters even worse.

Do I earn enough for my wages to be subjected to a garnishment?

There is a federal law known as the Consumer Credit Protection Act which limits the amount of wages that can be subject to garnishment. This law applies in all 50 states, the District of Columbia, and all U.S. territories and possessions. To determine how these limits apply in your situation, you must determine your "disposable" income. Basically, your disposable income is your total gross income minus all legally required deductions such as federal, state, and local taxes, Social Security (a/k/a FICA), and certain retirement deductions. The amount left after these deductions is your disposable income. You CANNOT deduct amounts for insurance, union dues, charitable contributions, and some types of retirement plan contributions or other purely voluntary deductions when calculating disposable income.

If your disposable income does not exceed $217.50 weekly, $435.00 biweekly, $471.25 semi-monthly, or $942.50 monthly, then your wages are fully exempt from garnishment and cannot be taken to satisfy a debt. However, if you get a raise and your wages exceed these exempt amounts, then a portion of your wages can be taken as calculated below.

You can calculate the amount that can be taken from you in a garnishment. First, determine how frequently you are paid. Weekly? Biweekly (every other week or 26 times per year)? Semi-monthly (always just twice per month or 24 times per year)? Monthly? Second, determine your disposable income as discussed above.

- If your disposable weekly income is more than $217.50 but less than $290.00, the amount of the garnishment is equal to the amount of your wages in excess of $217.50.
- If your disposable biweekly income is more than $435.00 but less than $580.00, the amount of the garnishment is equal to the amount of your wages in excess of $435.00.
- If your disposable semi-monthly income is more than $471.25 but less than $628.33, the amount of the garnishment is equal to the amount of your wages in excess of $471.25.
- If your disposable monthly income is more than $942.50 but less than $1,256.66, the amount of the garnishment is equal to the amount of your wages in excess of $942.50.

- If your disposable income is greater than $290.00 weekly, $580.00 biweekly, $628.33 semi-monthly, or $1,256.66 monthly, then the amount of the garnishment is equal to 25 percent of your disposable income.
- If the garnishment is to collect child support or alimony, the amount can be as much as 60 percent, plus an additional amount for any child support or alimony arrearage.

Remember, though, that wages are not your only asset that may be subject to garnishment. The fact that your wage income may not be enough to be subject to garnishment does not mean that other assets, like bank account balances, are not subject to garnishment.

Is the garnishment properly issued under state or other applicable law?

In most circumstances, a garnishment must be preceded by a court judgment. In other words, before the person you owe can garnish your wages or accounts, they must have first obtained a court judgment against you. Before any such judgment can be handed down, you must have been sued and given proper notice that you were being sued. So, if you've been hit out of the blue with a garnishment, it's possible that proper garnishment procedures have not been followed, and you may be able to defend yourself against the garnishment on this basis.

Again, this is not a defense that you can undertake yourself, and you will need competent legal advice. Also, be aware that certain types of creditors are not required to take you to court first. For example, if you are being garnished for student loan debt, your wages can be subject to an "administrative" wage garnishment. These procedures are governed by federal law and do not require a lawsuit or trip to court before your wages are taken.

It is possible, but not likely, that your garnishment was initiated in violation of state law. However, if you are certain that you never received any notice whatsoever of being sued and the debt you owe (or allegedly owe) is not subject to an "administrative" or other nonjudicial garnishment, you may have become a victim of a "debt buyer" type of lawsuit. With a little investigation, a competent debt relief lawyer can determine if this has happened to you. If so, you may have defenses to the garnishment based on problems with that particular type of lawsuit.

The primary advantage of examining whether the garnishment is proper under state or other applicable law is that, if you can successfully challenge the garnishment, you don't have to consider more drastic measures to deal with the situation.

The primary disadvantages to examining whether the garnishment is proper under state or applicable law include time and expense. By the time you receive notice of a garnishment, there is usually little additional time for competent legal counsel to investigate the validity of the garnishment. Any time spent investigating the validity of the garnishment effectively counts against you. And if it is determined that the garnishment was properly issued, you've spent valuable time and have nothing to show for it. In other words, you're still about to lose wages and/or money from your bank accounts because of the garnishment. Additionally, you will incur legal fees in having a competent debt relief lawyer look into the matter for you. Although these fees aren't likely to be very substantial, this money might be better spent elsewhere; if it turns out that the garnishment was validly issued, you don't get back those legal fees, and you're still at square one.

Does Chapter 7 bankruptcy or Chapter 13 debt consolidation have any effect on a garnishment?

Yes. Simply put, either of these formal debt relief options will instantly stop a garnishment no matter what your situation may be. And, it doesn't matter where you are in the garnishment process. For example, if the garnishment is in place and about to take effect, formal debt relief will stop it from taking effect at all. If the garnishment has already started, the garnishment must stop immediately upon the filing of a case under Chapter 7 or Chapter 13. This means that even if you have lost money to the garnishment in the past, you can prevent any more loss from occurring. Additionally, in Mississippi, and most states, a competent consumer bankruptcy lawyer can usually get back funds taken from you within a few days of the filing of your Chapter 7 or Chapter 13 case. One notable exception to immediately stopping the garnishment is where you've had two or more bankruptcy cases pending within one year of the date you file your case to stop the garnishment. But, even in such circumstances, a competent consumer bankruptcy lawyer will know how to take additional steps to protect you and your property from the garnishment.

An additional and substantial benefit you derive from formal debt relief under Chapter 7 or Chapter 13 is complete protection from ALL of your creditors, not just the creditor trying to garnish you. A Chapter 7 case completely eliminates most types of unsecured debt, while a Chapter 13 case allows you to formulate an affordable repayment plan that covers all your debt, not just the one that led to the garnishment. But either way, you are fully protected from the garnishment and all other debt collection attempts that might be directed toward you. And, at the end of your case, you are either completely debt-free or in much better financial shape than you were at the beginning.

So, the bottom line is that if you are facing a garnishment, get competent legal advice right away! You are most likely facing an imminent and significant loss of money or other property if you fail to take immediate and proper action. If you are facing a garnishment, we can arrange a free, emergency consultation for you to meet with one of our attorneys. Our attorneys are competent and experienced debt relief attorneys who can quickly and accurately assess your situation and take prompt action to protect you.

One final note about a nuanced issue with regard to a certain type of lawsuit. Sometimes our clients have been in car accidents where, unfortunately, they did not have car insurance. If they did not have insurance, oftentimes the party who was in the accident with them will file a lawsuit against them and, at the same time, try to have that person's driver's license suspended due to lack of insurance with the Secretary of

State. In that case, a bankruptcy filing with the car accident debt/lawsuit debt listed to be discharged can let the person who was uninsured get their driver's license back (as long as the accident was not caused by **nor** was there a criminal charge of driving under the influence of drugs or alcohol, or certain acts of negligence or wantonness). The person can get their driver's license back by simply paying a reinstatement fee to the applicable Secretary of State/driver's license department of their respective state.

Chapter 14

Divorce and Bankruptcy

Not surprisingly, the stress of debt and money issues is a leading cause of divorce in our country. Unfortunately, the interplay between divorce and bankruptcy is a common topic that comes up for many of our clients. The interplay is important, however, as most couples have joint debts, meaning that they both owe the third-party creditor on the debt. What does a separation or divorce do to the debt? Who is responsible for paying it? And who can be pursued if the debt is not paid? As a general rule, we advise couples who are in the unfortunate situation of thinking about or actually going through with a separation or divorce to consider a joint Chapter 7 bankruptcy filing if bankruptcy does become a consideration.

Is It Better to File for Bankruptcy Before or After a Divorce?
By Attorney Amy K. Tanner

This is truly not a yes or no question! Everyone's circumstances do vary, but there are a few scenarios that we see on a regular basis.

First of all, if you have found yourselves with a mountain of joint debt and on the verge of a divorce, our first recommendation is to seek advice on the benefit of filing a joint bankruptcy **before** the divorce. This can possibly save your marriage if the mounting debt is causing the majority of your marital strife, or it could provide you both with a total fresh start after divorce.

If you need to seek advice, individually or jointly, on filing for bankruptcy prior to a final divorce decree, it is important to inform your bankruptcy attorney that you are considering divorce. Your bankruptcy attorney can then give you the most intelligent advice on how to handle any individual or marital debts. It is also important to provide your divorce attorney with your bankruptcy information so that he or she can craft a decree that is in accord with the treatment of debts that you have chosen with your bankruptcy.

In many instances, one or both spouses are eventually driven to bankruptcy after the divorce is already final. This is not a problem, but you should be prepared to provide your bankruptcy attorney with a copy of your divorce decree. This can be helpful in crafting a successful bankruptcy case for you if there is language in the decree regarding how certain joint debts are to be handled.

Can I File Bankruptcy on Debts from a Divorce?
By Attorney Amy K. Tanner

Most divorce decrees and marital settlements will address the debts that exist at the time the parties separate. There is usually some type of division of the debt. Most couples have debt that turns out to be his, mine, and ours. The only party the creditor is interested in is the person who is actually liable on the debt. A creditor does not care if your divorce decree states that your ex-spouse should pay a debt that is in your name. The creditor is going to collect against the person who is named and liable on the debt itself, regardless of what is called a hold-harmless provision in a divorce decree.

The hold-harmless language is an indemnification provision that provides for the spouse who was assigned to pay a particular debt to do so, leaving the other marital party unharmed by the debt itself. The division of debt can become a real issue in bankruptcy. Even the hold-harmless indemnification can be a contingent debt in a bankruptcy. §523 of the United States Bankruptcy Code provides that any debt to a spouse or former spouse that arose during the dissolution of marriage is non-dischargeable in a Chapter 7 case. Although the spouse who files for bankruptcy can discharge the debt as to the creditor, he or she cannot discharge the obligation to hold the former spouse harmless.

If you have been through a divorce, it is very important that you are familiar with your obligations on any marital debt, especially if you are in a position of needing to seek bankruptcy assistance. This will allow you to get the best advice possible. The division of debt and whether or not there are any hold-harmless provisions in your divorce decree will be a factor in determining what will be the most helpful bankruptcy option to try and avoid any issues stemming from the marital settlement of debts.

Can Your Ex-Spouse Escape His or Her Financial Responsibilities Under a Divorce Decree or Other Domestic Support Order by Filing for Bankruptcy Relief?

By Attorney Carla Handy

After the emotional and financial turmoil of going through a divorce, there is nothing more frightening than being faced with the possibility that your ex-spouse may be able to avoid his or her financial responsibilities to you by seeking bankruptcy relief. The good news is that, for the most part, this will not be true. However, there are some exceptions to this general rule.

Let's start with the good news first. Regardless of whether your ex-spouse files a Chapter 7 or Chapter 13 bankruptcy petition, he or she will be unable to discharge (or get rid of) any obligation to you to pay a domestic support obligation, and this will include alimony or child support. Under the 2005 amendments to the Bankruptcy Code, Congress declared any obligation that is in the nature of alimony, maintenance, and support to be non-dischargeable in a Chapter 7 or Chapter 13. Congress defined a domestic support obligation as any debt arising before, during, or after the filing of a bankruptcy petition, owed to a spouse, former spouse, or child, that is in the nature of alimony, maintenance, or support and has been established by a legally binding agreement or court order such as a divorce decree. If a debt is labeled as alimony or child support in a divorce decree or other court order, there is no question that the debtor will have to continue to pay this financial responsibility. However, there can be other obligations such as the requirement to pay the monthly mortgage payment or car payment required by a court order where a question of dischargeability can arise. The answer of whether this financial obligation was intended to be in the nature of alimony, maintenance, or support is critical in making the debt non-dischargeable.

What is trickier is the question of whether the obligation under a divorce decree to pay things other than alimony or child support is dischargeable. These are commonly described as property settlement issues. One example would include an order to pay a third party for a debt that arose during the marriage such as a credit card debt in the joint names of the husband and wife. If the obligation to pay the credit card arises from a divorce decree or separation agreement, then the obligation will not be dischargeable in a Chapter 7. It may, however, still be dischargeable in a Chapter 13 pursuant to the super discharge afforded to debtors who file under that chapter of the Bankruptcy Code.

Other protections afforded to a spouse or child by the Bankruptcy Code include the requirement that each alimony or child support payment that falls due after the filing of a Chapter 13 bankruptcy petition must be paid or the debtor will be denied an overall discharge in the case. Arrearage claims for alimony or child support must be paid in full by the debtor in a Chapter 13 case unless the creditor spouse agrees otherwise. Finally, the bankruptcy court can refuse to approve a Chapter 13 plan if the debtor is not current on domestic support obligations.

Chapter 15

Taxes and Bankruptcy

Another important topic that comes up repeatedly with many of our clients is with regard to taxes and how they are affected by a bankruptcy filing, either Chapter 7 or Chapter 13. Contrary to popular belief, taxes can be discharged in bankruptcy, assuming that certain rules and qualifications are met. Tax debt can also be paid back through a Chapter 13 debt consolidation plan. The IRS and state taxing authorities have many enforcement mechanisms and procedures to ensure payment, and they can put these enforcement actions into place quickly to the great detriment of the consumer. As a result, if you have tax debt or concerns that you are confronting, please be aware of your rights under the Bankruptcy Code. There is also interplay with taxes when property is forgiven or settled short of the full balance owed being paid.

What Impact Does Filing for Bankruptcy Have on My Back Taxes?
By Attorney Amy K. Tanner

First of all, if you are contemplating filing any form of bankruptcy, it is imperative that you are up to date with filing all of your federal tax returns with the Internal Revenue Service, and it is strongly recommended that you keep legible copies of **all** of your federal tax returns that have been filed.

Sometimes the issue is that you have not been able to pay your federal, state, or other tax debt. This is when a Chapter 13 bankruptcy can really help you. In most cases, an individual can include to be paid in a Chapter 13 plan all back tax debt that they have not been able to pay. There can be quite a few benefits to handling back tax debt in a Chapter 13. The automatic stay that goes into effect immediately upon the filing of a Chapter 13 bankruptcy can stop the Internal Revenue Service from freezing future refunds that come due to you. (See my blog post from September 24, 2012 at www.bondandbotes.com for more information on the automatic stay.) An additional benefit of including and paying past due tax debt in a Chapter 13 debt consolidation plan is that in most cases, interest and penalties stop accruing on the pre-petition tax debt included in the Chapter 13 Plan.

Generally, back tax debt is non-dischargeable in any form of bankruptcy. However, in some instances back tax debt can be determined dischargeable (wiped out). There are quite a few factors involved, and this can be a more tedious and complicated process. It is best to seek the assistance of legal counsel to determine how to best help you with your back tax debt.

Can Tax Debt Be Discharged in Bankruptcy?
By Attorney Amy K. Tanner

Contrary to general belief, you can discharge tax debt in a bankruptcy if the tax debt meets certain and specific criteria. Some of the initial questions to ask are whether the tax returns are deemed filed, what constitutes a tax return, and when was the tax assessed.

Basic Rules of Tax Discharge

There are five basic rules of tax discharge. First, there is the three-year rule. The tax return must have been due and filed more than three years prior to the date of filing the bankruptcy. Next, there is the 240-day rule. This means that the tax must have been assessed more than 240 days prior to the bankruptcy filing date. In conjunction to this rule, there is the two-year rule, which depends on when the taxes were filed in relation to the date you are filing for bankruptcy or whether you failed to file a return at all. The final two rules may seem a little obvious. They are the no-fraud tax return rule and the no tax evasion rule.

There are many complexities within these five basic rules. For instance, you may have had an event that has caused tolling of the aforementioned time periods, such as a previous bankruptcy, installment agreement, or an offer in compromise. These events can extend the statute of limitation on discharging the tax debt in a bankruptcy. These time limitations must be carefully calculated.

There are also a few types of tax debt that are simply not dischargeable. These include trust fund taxes; however, the collection of trust fund taxes may be subject to a statute of limitations, and taxes for civil penalties.

As mentioned, determining if your federal tax debt is dischargeable in bankruptcy is a complex calculation and deserves careful analysis. Our attorneys can help you through this analysis and, if the tax debt is not appropriate to discharge, we may be able to assist you with other tax resolutions such as an installment agreement or offers in compromise.

Will I Be Able to Keep My Tax Refund Each Year If I File a Chapter 13 Bankruptcy?

By Attorney Carla M. Handy

Chapter 13 is considered the debt consolidation chapter of the Bankruptcy Code for individuals with regular income. As such, a debtor is paying back creditors over an extended period of time, through a three- or five-year repayment plan. Debtors are often concerned about whether they will be required to turn over their tax refunds each year during this Chapter 13 repayment plan. The short answer is maybe.

In certain bankruptcy districts or divisions, the Chapter 13 trustee may review the debtor's tax return each year and, if a refund is due, modify the Chapter 13 plan to require the refund be paid into the plan.

In other districts or divisions, the trustee will never ask for this review, and the debtor will be able to keep the yearly refund. An experienced bankruptcy attorney will be able to advise you whether the Chapter 13 trustee in your district or division will require you to turn over your refund each year. If you happen to reside in a district or division where you will be required to turn over your tax refund to the Chapter 13 plan, there is a solution. You can simply adjust the withholding taxes from your paycheck to receive more of your wages each pay period instead of receiving it back in a tax refund once a year. This method will take some planning on your part, but with the help of a tax advisor and your bankruptcy attorney, it can provide a satisfactory solution to the problem.

Can I Be Taxed on Forgiveness of Debt or for Debts Discharged in Bankruptcy or for Deficiency Balance on My Home and What Should I Do If I Received a 1099 Issued to the IRS for Debt?

By Attorney Ronald C. Sykstus

Many of our clients present us with these questions, especially during tax season. The simple answer to these questions is…maybe…

This area of questions is actually quite complicated. If you find yourself presented with these types of questions, we recommend seeking the assistance of your tax advisor or a tax professional.

To give you an overview of this area, I will address these areas one issue at a time.

The first question is what happens if you settle a debt and pay the debt collector or creditor less than what you owe? Many times, debt collectors will try to coerce a settlement from someone, claiming that the person owes money but that they will accept less than what is owed, and this will supposedly settle the debt in full. Please make sure that is the case if you try this tactic and obtain this agreement in writing. Oftentimes, debt collectors and debt buyers will simply sell the difference of what you didn't pay to another debt collector who will then tell you that the debt was not settled in full. Additionally, the first debt collector with whom you settled can issue a 1099 forgiveness of debt to the IRS, and that difference will be taxable income to you. By way of example, let's say a debt collector says you owe $10,000. You are not sure exactly what you owe or even what the debt is about. Many times, however, when people are harassed in this manner, they will want to put this perceived issue behind them. Let's say the debt collector says, "Pay us $5,000 today and we will forgive 50 percent of the debt. You settle it that day and then the debt collector will submit to the IRS and copy you with a 1099 showing that you received $5,000 in "income" for the forgiveness of debt.

First of all, when you settle debts in this manner, make sure that you write on the memo section of the check "for full and complete satisfaction of all debts and accounts between John Doe and ABC Debt Collector for XYZ creditor account #123…" (spell out your full name and the debt collector and the underlying creditor, account number, etc.). This will give the debt collector some problems if and when the debt collector tries to sell the debt later on to another debt buyer. Additionally, there is a question as to whether a 1099 should issue for disputed debts. Make it clear in writing also if you dispute a debt and settle it with "reservation of all rights." At least that way, you have given your tax advisor a fighting chance as to whether this is really taxable income to you. The settlement of debts, however, is a very tricky area, and you would be well advised to discuss any strategy with an attorney and a tax advisor before you actually embark on this type of plan.

The second issue is what if you get a 1099 for debt forgiveness and you file bankruptcy on that particular debt? The good news is that the IRS has already considered this matter and has issued a form to be submitted, IRS form 982, which deals with debts that were discharged in bankruptcy or where a person is insolvent. If you have filed bankruptcy and you receive a 1099 from various creditors and debt collectors that were listed and discharged in your bankruptcy, please use this form to address the 1099(s) you received and also bring it to your tax advisor or tax professional to address in the filing of your tax return.

Finally, what can a person do if he or she sold their principal residence as a short sale and the lender issued a 1099 for the difference forgiven? Are taxes required to be paid on that difference? The Mortgage Forgiveness Debt Relief Act was enacted to cover this situation through the end of tax year 2013, so that should allow someone in this circumstance to avoid being taxed. There was some talk in Congress about extending this law, but as of the date of this book, it has not been extended. Please check with the IRS and your tax advisor if this issue applies to you. Of course, if you filed for bankruptcy and surrendered your home in bankruptcy, then the IRS form 982 (debtor insolvency form) addresses this issue for you.

This is just a general overview of these topics as, again, these questions come up repeatedly during tax season and can be quite complicated. With regard to debt settlements, please contact our office to talk to one of our consumer lawyers with regard to your personal financial situation. If you have specific questions that are limited to the taxable consequences for other debt forgiveness and the receipt of 1099s for debt, please contact your tax advisor or your tax professional or preparer.

Should You File a Tax Return If You Owe the IRS Money and Can't Afford to Pay?
By Attorney Mary Conner Pool

YES, it is extremely important that you file a tax return on time to avoid having penalties assessed against you. If you cannot afford to pay the IRS in one lump sum, pay as much as you can with the return. By filing your tax return on time, you avoid having a late filing penalty fee assessed by the IRS. In addition, you will be able to reduce the amount of interest assessed when you pay as much as you can afford when filing your tax return.

If you cannot afford to pay the full amount due, it is best to try to set up a payment agreement with the IRS by completing IRS Form 9465-FS and sending it to the IRS with your tax return. This will let the IRS know that you are interested in paying your remaining tax liabilities through installment payments.

Filing a Chapter 13 would allow you to pay the liability over a five-year period, and by filing Chapter 7 you may be able to discharge older tax debts if certain criteria are met. For example, if you have assessed tax liabilities for multiple years and have filed your tax returns on time, the Bankruptcy Code may allow for some of those tax liabilities to be discharged. Therefore, it is extremely important to timely file your tax returns.

Chapter 16

Student Loans and Bankruptcy

As of 2013, the outstanding student loan debt in our country exceeded the total amount of debt that is due on credit cards. The total amount of student loan debt now exceeds one trillion dollars. Unfortunately, this is a topic that comes up repeatedly. The question is what can you do with student loan debt and is it dischargeable in bankruptcy? The technical answer is yes, student loan debt is dischargeable in bankruptcy under the hardship provision of the Bankruptcy Code, but it is a very difficult standard to meet. Additionally, if people are in default on student loan debts and are having administrative garnishments on their wages, if their tax refunds are seized or they are undergoing collection harassment for student loan debt, another possibility is Chapter 13 bankruptcy.

Let's start with the Chapter 7 discharge provision of the Bankruptcy Code to see what that looks like:

11 U.S.C. § 523(a)(8). Section 523(a)(8) reads as follows:

(a) A discharge under section 727...does not discharge an individual debtor from any debt–

* * * *

(8) unless excepting such debt from discharge under this paragraph would impose an undue hardship on the debtor and the debtor's dependents, for --

(A) (i) an educational benefit overpayment or loan made, insured, or guaranteed by a governmental unit, or made under any program funded in whole or in part by a governmental unit or nonprofit institution; or

(ii) an obligation to repay funds received as an educational benefit, scholarship, or stipend; or

(B) any other educational loan that is a qualified educational loan, as defined in section 221(d)(1) of the Internal Revenue Code of 1986, incurred by a debtor who is an individual[.]

Although the Bankruptcy Code does not define the term "undue hardship" for purposes of § 523(a)(8), many courts have adopted the standard for determining same as set forth in *Brunner v. New York State Higher Educ. Servs. Corp. (In re Brunner),* 831 F.2d 395 (2d Cir. 1987). To establish undue hardship, the *Brunner* standard requires the debtor to prove by a preponderance of the evidence:

(1) that the debtor cannot maintain, based on current income and expenses, a "minimal" standard of living for [himself] and [his] dependents if forced to repay the loans; (2) that additional circumstances exist indicating that this state of affairs is likely to persist for a significant portion of the repayment period of the student loans.

This is such a difficult standard to meet, in part, due to the fact that there are many administrative ways and circumstances in which someone can work out a repayment plan, even sometimes at zero dollars per month, in order to pay back a student loan debt over time. In our opinion, this is also complicated by the fact that most student loan debt is government-guaranteed debt, and politics then creates a complicating factor here as well as far as discharging these types of debt.

The other option a person may have is to pay back student loan debts either in full or in part in a Chapter 13 bankruptcy plan of reorganization. The positive aspect of doing it this way is that any collection activity and administrative wage garnishment from a person's paycheck would stop.

Can I Find Out the Status of My Government Student Loans?
By Attorney Ronald C. Sykstus

Many times clients will come to us and say that they are being called about student loans, and they have no idea about any student loans they may owe. For most people, student loans were obtained years ago, and the paperwork for the student loans has long since been misplaced or lost. For any federal government student loans, please visit the following website: www.nslds.ed.gov. At this site you will need to request a pin number. Be sure to safeguard your personal pin number. This will allow you to get all of your federal government student loan information. It will show what you owe as far as student loan debt and to whom you owe it. Please ensure that you make a copy of all of the student loan information once you get it and keep it in a safe place.

If you do not have access to the Internet, you can also call a toll-free number at 1-800-433-3243 to get your student loan information. However, the best and most complete way is by visiting the website www.nslds.ed.gov. Of course, if you have not already obtained your free credit reports, as you are allowed to obtain all of them once per year, please get all of your free credit reports at www.annualcreditreport.com.

Student Loan Debt Becoming Increasingly Common in Bankruptcies
By Attorney Grant McNutt

The economy is extremely tough right now. It is not only in the back of everyone's minds, but it is also the number one political topic, and for good reason. It seems like every single family has had to deal with financial hardship in some way, whether income was reduced, a job was lost, work hours were increased without pay increase, or a loved one came upon hard times.

There is one group who the economy has hit much harder than others though: graduating students.

A national bankruptcy lawyers' group has warned that many new graduates are beginning to find that jobs are not nearly as easy to find as they were expecting, and when that is added to the rapidly increasing amount of student loan debt required to graduate, students could be facing an economic crisis that rivals even the mortgage bust of recent years.

According to the National Association of Consumer Bankruptcy Attorneys, of the over 850 bankruptcy lawyers surveyed, four out of five said that new potential clients with student debt have become "somewhat" or "significantly" more common in just the past three to four years.

One-quarter of all respondents said that the number of potential clients with student loan debt has increased by over 50 percent, while a third said that it had increased by 25-50 percent.

The unfortunate reality is that student loan debt is rarely ever forgiven in bankruptcy filings, and student loan providers are generally less flexible in offering repayment assistance than regular credit card companies.

Many lawmakers are looking into ways to change this legislation that would be beneficial to lenders and borrowers, as well as taxpayers.

Consequences of Defaulting on a Student Loan
By Attorney Joshua Lawhorn

A major financial problem in the United States today is student loan debt. College tuition is sharply increasing, while the average salary remains stagnant. Many college graduates have difficulty finding a job in their field of study or at all. During this difficult time, one thing remains: student loans. While deferment and forbearance programs are an option, those possibilities often fail, and the interest on the loans continues to add more to what is owed. Once the few options available are exhausted, borrowers unable to pay can default on their student loans. After default, both government-guaranteed and private student loan lenders have options available to collect on defaulted student loans.

One option available is wage garnishment. The government-guaranteed student loans can garnish up to 15 percent of your disposable income per pay period and can continue the garnishment until the loan is paid in full. Also, a government-guaranteed or private student loan lender can choose to file a lawsuit against you. Once a judgment is entered, there are several options available to collect on the loan. The lender can also add court costs and attorney's fees associated with the lawsuit.

Government-guaranteed student loan lenders can also intercept your state or federal tax refund. Many people rely on their tax refunds each year, only to have it offset due to a defaulted student loan. This is a fairly common method that government-guaranteed lenders use to collect after default.

If you receive social security disability or retirement benefits, government-guaranteed lenders can garnish 15 percent of your benefits. This is one of the few situations in which social security benefits can be garnished.

If you are currently in default or in danger of default on your student loans, you do have options, but you need to act quickly.

Chapter 17

Business Bankruptcy – Chapter 11

What Is Chapter 11 Business Bankruptcy?
By Attorney Amy K. Tanner

Many clients I meet with regarding bankruptcy ask me, "What is a Chapter 11 bankruptcy case?" A Chapter 11 bankruptcy allows an individual or a business to reorganize debts while being protected from creditors.

The filing of a Chapter 11 petition automatically stays all foreclosure, collection actions, civil litigation, and creditor actions of any kind. The debtor must file a voluntary petition to commence a Chapter 11 case, including the names and addresses of its creditors and owners, a description of its property and assets, and its financial condition.

Anyone except a government agency, estate, non-business trust, stockbroker, commodity broker, insurance company, bank, or SBA-licensed small business investment company can file under Chapter 11. The Chapter 11 filing fee is generally higher than the filing fee for other chapters of bankruptcy. In addition, there is a quarterly fee paid to the Bankruptcy Administrator's office based on the amount disbursed during each quarter by the debtor. The Bankruptcy Administrator's office for the Northern District, Northern Division of Alabama provides a schedule for such quarterly fees at the following link: http://www.alnba.uscourts.gov/NewChapter11QuarterlyFees.pdf.

A Chapter 11 debtor is known as a "debtor-in-possession" after the petition is filed. Generally, no trustee is appointed by the court, and the debtor-in-possession is responsible for filing monthly operating reports, paying the quarterly fees, and preparing and filing its plan of reorganization. A trustee may be appointed by the bankruptcy court, however, if requested by the bankruptcy administrator or creditors. If the debtor is a business, it may continue to operate but must comply with the requirements of the bankruptcy law and courts to do so.

After the filing of the voluntary petition, the debtor must prepare and file a disclosure statement informing the court and its creditors of the history or background of the debtor and its business, its current financial condition, and its plan for reorganization. This statement acts as a tool to inform the creditors of the causes of the bankruptcy and the debtor's plans to reorganize its business and deal with its debts and taxes.

After approval of the disclosure statement by the court, the debtor files a Chapter 11 plan that is then voted on by the creditors. Upon acceptance by the creditors and approval by the court, the plan is "confirmed." The confirmation of the plan terminates the bankruptcy estate and title to property that is retained reverts back to the reorganized debtor. The debtor and all parties are bound to the terms of the confirmed plan. It is, in essence, a new agreement for the rehabilitation of the debtor and the handling of its debts.

A Chapter 11 case allows you to reschedule your debts, possibly cancel leases and other executory contracts, and sell, with court permission, nonproductive assets while under bankruptcy protection. A Chapter 11 case could be an excellent tool for a viable business or an individual who exceeds the debt limits under Chapter 13 to restructure debts and move forward.

Chapter 18

Family Farmer and Family Fisherman Reorganization – Chapter 12

Chapter 12 – Family Farmer and Family Fisherman Reorganization
By Attorney Carla Handy

These three articles cover a specialized chapter under the Bankruptcy Code for farmers and fishermen.

Farmers have been the backbone of this country since its inception. As a result of the special place they hold in our society and economy, a specific chapter in the Bankruptcy Code was created by Congress to assist family farmers and family fishermen in reorganizing their debt. This chapter of the Bankruptcy Code recognizes the inherent risks associated with farming for a living, including unpredictable weather and market conditions, and provides a unique avenue for farmers to restructure their debt load.

Chapter 12 of the Bankruptcy Code was first included as a temporary provision in 1986, and for many years its temporary nature required Congress to pass extensions in order to continue providing this relief to farmers. The 2005 amendments to the Bankruptcy Code, known as BAPCPA, made this relief for farmers permanent and added family fishermen as a category of debtors who were entitled to relief under the chapter.

Chapter 12 has the unique feature of combining both consumer and commercial bankruptcy theories that allow family farmers to restructure their debt over an extended period of time. A number of the initial qualification requirements under Chapter 12 are similar to the qualification requirements under Chapter 13, which is used by individual consumers to adjust debt. One of the first qualification requirements for an individual family farmer is to complete pre-filing credit counseling. This requirement is critical because a case is subject to immediate dismissal unless the debtor farmer has filed a certificate of completion of this credit counseling. An experienced bankruptcy attorney will be able to assist a family farmer or fisherman in obtaining this counseling prior to filing a Chapter 12 bankruptcy petition.

To qualify to file under Chapter 12, an individual farmer or fisherman must actually be engaged in a farming or fishing operation that provides at least 50 percent of that person's gross income for the preceding year or in each of the two years preceding. The farmer's total debt cannot exceed 3.2 million dollars, and at least 50 percent of the farmer's debt, generally, must have arisen as a result of the farming operation. The total amounts of debt and income requirements differ slightly for family fishermen. Most farmers who find themselves in financial difficulty will usually qualify under these requirements, but a bankruptcy attorney experienced in filing under Chapter 12 is needed to insure all requirements are met.

Cash Collateral and the Family Farmer
By Attorney Carla Handy

Now let's discuss an issue of critical importance to the success of a Chapter 12 case—the farmer's ability to use cash collateral to pay creditors and the expenses of the ongoing farming operation. In most Chapter 12 cases, the debtors will come in to the case owing substantial debt on the farm real estate and farming equipment. The financing documents of the lender bank securing the repayment of this debt will often include language granting the lender bank a lien in the proceeds of the farmer's crop, flock, or herd when same is sold at market. Often the farmer will have given the lender bank an assignment on the sale proceeds which allows the bank to obtain payment on its debt before the remaining balance of the sale proceeds are turned over to the farmer. This lien against the sale proceeds creates an issue as to whether the farmer can use the sale proceeds after the filing of the Chapter 12 bankruptcy petition to pay operational expenses of the farm and other creditors.

Upon filing the Chapter 12 bankruptcy petition, the farmer will propose a plan to pay back his creditors over time, and that repayment plan will require approval by the bankruptcy judge. But before this approval occurs, creditors will want to receive some form of payment in the interim. As a secured creditor, a lender bank is entitled to have the debt secured by the farmland and equipment adequately protected against depreciation of the assets once the bank's stream of payments on the debt is interrupted by the filing of the Chapter 12 bankruptcy petition. In addition, because the lender bank has a lien against the sale proceeds of the farm product, the farmer must obtain permission from the bankruptcy court to use this cash collateral for farm expenses and paying other creditors. As a result of these two requirements of the Bankruptcy Code, the farmer and the lender bank must come to an agreement as to the use of the cash collateral, or the bankruptcy judge will be required to issue an order as to how the money is to be used prior to the Chapter 12 plan being approved.

Clearly, an agreement between the farmer and the lender bank is preferred, as a bird in the hand is better than one in the bush. But in the event an agreement cannot be reached and the bankruptcy judge must decide the issue, it is important for the farmer to have a detailed list of the monthly farm expenses to present to the court. In this farm budget special attention should be paid to the payment of vendors necessary to the continued operation of the farm. Examples of these critical vendors would include propane providers and the electric and water utilities and whether these vendors will be willing to extend post-petition credit or will require cash on delivery.

An attorney experienced in filing Chapter 12 bankruptcies will be able to assist a family farmer or fisherman in navigating the often contentious path of satisfying the lender bank while retaining sufficient monies to fund ongoing farm operations.

Long-Term Farm Debt and the Family Farmer
By Attorney Carla Handy

The final issue to review is how long-term farm debt can be addressed in a Chapter 12 plan. In most Chapter 12 cases, the debtors will come in to the case owing substantial debt on the farm real estate and farming equipment. How much time a farmer will have through a Chapter 12 repayment plan to pay back this debt is an issue that is critical to the success of a Chapter 12 case. Generally speaking, unsecured debt and priority debt (e.g., income tax liability) must be paid within a five-year period. Secured debt, however, like the large indebtedness owed on the farm, can be extended out over a much longer period of time.

Let's take an example of a poultry farm that also contains, in addition to the poultry houses, the farmer's residential home. Let's say further that the farmer borrowed $750,000 to purchase the farm five years ago, and that debt was amortized over 15 years at an interest rate of 10 percent. Finally, let's assume the farm acreage, residential home, and poultry houses are now worth only $500,000 after the market downturn. Potentially, a Chapter 12 repayment plan could be crafted to pay the farm debt to the extent of the $500,000 value over 20 years at 6 percent interest, with the remaining balance treated as other unsecured debt would be treated in the plan. This could be a significant savings for the farmer, and the Bankruptcy Code does allow for such treatment of long-term secured debt.

There are some caveats to this type of plan treatment for long-term secured debt. The proposed treatment must comply with Section 1225 of the Bankruptcy Code, which requires a plan to be proposed in good faith. A bankruptcy judge will evaluate the proposed plan on this basis and, in making the good faith determination, can consider the current market for both term and interest rate. While the Chapter

12 repayment plan does not have to mirror the current market terms, a Chapter 12 bankruptcy attorney will bear the current terms in mind in crafting a confirmable Chapter 12 plan. An attorney experienced in filing Chapter 12 bankruptcies will be able to assist a family farmer or fisherman in proposing a Chapter 12 plan that can provide a long-term repayment period on the farm debt while still complying with the requirement of the Bankruptcy Code.

CHAPTER 19

MISCELLANEOUS CONSUMER LAWS THAT EVERYONE SHOULD KNOW

A. Fair Debt Collection Practices Act (FDCPA)

Fair Debt Collection Practices Act (FDCPA)
By Attorney Ronald C. Sykstus

The Fair Debt Collection Practices Act (FDCPA) is found at 15 USC § 1692. It is a powerful federal consumer statute packed into just six pages. The FDCPA was enacted by Congress on September 20, 1977 and became effective six months later. In formulating the Act, Congress articulated the purposes for the enactment of legislation as follows: "There is abundant evidence of the use of abusive, deceptive, and unfair debt collection practices by many debt collectors. Abusive debt collection practices contribute to the number of personal bankruptcies, to marital instability, to the loss of jobs, and to the invasions of individual privacy." 15 USC § 1692(a).

For there to be a violation of this Act, there must be a consumer, a consumer debt, a debt collector, and a violation of the Act. It is important to note that this Act covers consumer debts only and does not cover commercial or business debts. The debt has to be for personal, family, or household purposes such as medical bills, utility bills, insurance bills, or credit cards. The following areas DO NOT fall under the FDCPA: child support, income tax, or tort claims such as car accidents. The debt collector involved must be a third-party debt collector. Note that the original creditor itself is excluded from the definition of a debt collector and, again, the Act only applies to a third-party debt collector or debt collection lawyers who have a regular debt collection practice.

Whether the communication or other conduct by a debt collector violates the FDCPA is determined by the courts by analyzing it from the perspective of the least sophisticated consumer to ensure that the FDCPA protects all consumers, the gullible as well as the shrewd. There are four keys in deciding whether there is a violation of the FDCPA: Was the communication untruthful, unfair, undignified, or disrespectful? Whether the debt is actually owed or not is immaterial.

If you believe you are being unfairly harassed by a third-party debt collector under the FDCPA, please feel free to contact one of our offices closest to you, as we practice in this area of law. Additionally, please use search engines such as Google or Bing to see who is contacting you and, if at all possible, get the full name of the debt collector as well as the full mailing address, city, state, and zip code. Additionally, it is very important to keep detailed notes if you start getting harassed in an untruthful, unfair, undignified, or disrespectful manner by a debt collector. Please write up detailed notes every time you are contacted in this disrespectful manner, and make sure you write down the time of the call, the date, the number the call came from, how the person identified himself or herself, and exactly what was said by them and by you. It is also very important to make sure you keep all correspondence received from the debt collector.

How Can I Stop a Debt Collector from Harassing Me?
By Attorney Ronald C. Sykstus

The Fair Debt Collection Practices Act is a federal law which proscribes and restricts a number of actions that debt collectors, collection agencies, and lawyers can take if they are pursuing you on a debt. Debt collectors, collection agencies, and lawyers are not allowed to harass you or abuse you in trying to collect a debt. Specifically, they cannot harass, oppress, or abuse anyone, they cannot threaten use of violence or other criminal means, and they cannot use profane or other abusive language in order to collect a debt.

The other way debt collectors, collection agencies, and lawyers will try to collect a debt from you is by writing a letter. They are required to specify certain things in what is called a 30-day validation notice. What they do is give you 30 days to dispute the debt. If you do dispute the debt or do not believe you owe it, or you have no idea what they are talking about, you have an absolute right to refuse to pay the debt and ask the collector to cease and stop all communication with you. In order to stop communication, you can write a letter back to the debt collector that says you dispute the debt, that you refuse to pay the debt, and that they are not allowed to contact you anymore either by phone or in writing. You will need to write it in your own writing, preferably by computer or handwriting if it is very legible, and please make sure you sign it, date it, and mail it to the debt collector, collection agency, or lawyer by certified mail, return receipt requested.

Please make sure you keep a copy of all communications that you both receive and send and that you also keep a log to keep track of any communication you get, especially after you send this dispute letter. Also, **please ensure that you keep a copy of the certified mail, return receipt acknowledgment so that you can verify** the debt collector, collection agency, or lawyer has received your letter.

B. Fair Credit Reporting Act (FCRA)

Fair Credit Reporting Act (FCRA)
By Attorney Ronald C. Sykstus

Everything that relates to a credit report for a consumer in our country is governed by a federal law called the Fair Credit Reporting Act. It is also referred to as the FCRA. This federal law is found at 15 USC § 1681. Pursuant to this law, the FCRA regulates the permissible information, access, accuracy, and compliance requirements of consumer credit reports. A consumer report is defined under this law as any written, oral, or other communication of any information by a consumer reporting agency bearing on a consumer's credit worthiness, credit standing, credit capacity, character, general reputation, personal characteristics, or mode of living which is used or expected to be used or collected in whole or in part for the purpose of serving as a factor in establishing the consumer's eligibility for credit or insurance to be used primarily for personal, family, or household purposes; employment purposes. 15 USC § 1681a(d)(1).

The FCRA further defines the exact definition of a consumer reporting agency: any person who, for monetary fees, dues, or on a cooperative nonprofit basis, regularly engages in whole or in part in the practice of assembling or evaluating consumer credit information or other information on consumers for the purpose of furnishing consumer reports to third parties, and uses any means or facility of interstate commerce for the purpose of preparing or furnishing consumer reports. 15 USC § 1681a(f).

The basic requirement under the FCRA provides that consumer reporting agencies must follow reasonable procedures to assure maximum possible accuracy of the information in a credit report. When Congress formulated this law, it noted that the FCRA was enacted in order to protect consumers against "the trend toward... the establishment of all sorts of computerized data banks [that placed a consumer] in great danger of having his life and character reduced to impersonal 'blips' and key punch holes in a stolid and unthinking machine which can literally ruin his reputation without cause." 116 Cong. Rec. 36570.

The FCRA is a complicated law, but it is an important one for consumers to know. This is the law a person who has received a bankruptcy discharge will most definitely want to use to improve his or her credit (which is possible!) after the bankruptcy is finished.

How Can I Dispute Incorrect or Erroneous Information on My Credit Report? By Attorney Ronald C. Sykstus

The law that applies for everything as it relates to a credit report and, specifically, how to dispute incorrect or erroneous information on your credit report is found under the Fair Credit Reporting Act (FCRA). The start point is to get your free credit reports **only in writing** and exactly as described previously in this book **in writing only** by submitting the form you can get and print from www.annualcreditreport.com and **mailing it into the annual credit report address in Atlanta.** Failure to get your credit report in this manner may prohibit you from getting resolution on your credit reports because you may enter into binding arbitration. **For credit report disputes, do not ever get your credit reports online—only get them in writing!**

The proper way to dispute something on your credit report is to dispute it **directly** with the credit reporting agency that shows the incorrect information (Equifax, Experian, or TransUnion). Please ensure that you MAIL your dispute letter by **certified mail, return receipt requested** so that you can verify that the letter was actually received by the credit reporting agency. Please also KEEP COPIES of ALL of your letters and all documents and enclosures that you send and receive. You may send a dispute letter to each credit reporting agency (CRA) from which you have ordered, received, and reviewed a copy of your credit report if you think there are errors or incorrect information.

A sample dispute letter looks something like what is set forth as follows. Please make sure you create your own form and tailor it to your exact problem or dispute.

Date
Certified Mail, Return Receipt Requested

Your name
Your address
Your city, state, zip code

Complaint Department
Name of Credit Report Agency *(TransUnion, Equifax, Experian)*
Address
City, state, zip code

Dear Sir/Ma'am:

After reviewing my credit report, I am writing to dispute the following information. I have circled the disputed items on my attached report. These include *(list item(s) disputed by name of source, such as creditors, and identify type of item, such as credit account, judgment, etc.)* This *item(s) is(are)* inaccurate because *(list exactly why each item is incorrect or incomplete).* Supporting documents have been enclosed. Pursuant to the FCRA, please forward them to the credit furnishers. If you are not going to forward them, please inform me immediately so that I may do so myself.

Sincerely, *Your name*

Encl. *(List what you are enclosing)*

You **must** dispute the incorrect information with the credit report agency itself and **NOT** the furnisher of the incorrect information. This is a fundamental concept under this law.

C. Telephone Consumer Protection Act (TCPA)

Telephone Consumer Protection Act (TCPA)
By Attorney Ronald C. Sykstus

The federal Telephone Consumer Protection Act of 1991 (TCPA) is found at 47 U.S.C. § 227. There are several subsections to the Act which authorize the FCC (Federal Communications Commission) to adopt rules, including the popular national "Do Not Call" list registry and other FCC rules that go beyond the substantive provisions in the statute.

There is a general restriction in the TCPA on auto-dialers and prerecorded messages. The TCPA prohibits making any call using an automatic dialing system or an artificial or pre-recorded voice to make any call to an emergency telephone line, a patient or guest room at a nursing home, hospital, or similar health facility, or a pager, cellular phone, or other service in which the called party is charged for the call. The prohibition against auto-dialing of cellular phone numbers applies to both text and voice messages. Live telephone solicitations to wireless subscribers are not prohibited, but subscribers can place their cellular telephone number on the Do Not Call list.

The Act explicitly grants consumers the right to bring suit for violations in state court. As far as relief, consumers can seek an injunction and/or the greater of actual monetary loss or up to $500 for each violation. The court may treble the damages if it finds that the defendant's actions were willful and knowing. The plaintiff must prove that the violation was done willfully or knowingly, but need not prove both. Furthermore, whether the defendant acts knowingly is relevant only to an enhanced award, and is not a general prerequisite to a recovery of statutory damages.

The statutory damage award is intended both as compensation and as a deterrent, and is not so disproportionate to actual damages as to violate due process, including in class actions. The consumer need not prove any monetary loss or actual damages in order to recover the statutory penalty because such losses are likely to be minimal, and a statutory penalty is necessary to motivate consumers to enforce the statute. The TCPA is a strict liability statute. The TCPA's substantive restrictions apply to any person, a term that includes individuals, partnerships, associations, joint stock companies, trusts, and corporations. The fact that an independent contractor actually places the calls does not insulate the principal from liability.

The area where we see a problem for our consumer clients is generally when they receive unsolicited calls or texts to their cells phones that they did not previously authorize.

How Can I Stop Telemarketing and Solicitation Calls to My Home and Cell Phone?
By Attorney Ronald C. Sykstus

The Telephone Consumer Protection Act (TCPA) is a powerful law that regulates telephone calls to both a home and cell phone. Specifically, 47 U.S.C. § 227(c)(5) sets forth the Do Not Call (DNC) list that is now common knowledge in our country. You can go to the government Do Not Call Registry located at www.donotcall.gov. You can register up to three numbers on the website, so make sure, even if you have to submit separate emails, that you register all of your home and cell phone numbers. You will then receive an email confirmation of the registration. It is very important that you actually print this document and save it in a safe place as it would be an exhibit if you had to enforce your rights to stop telemarketers from calling you.

The DNC provision of the TCPA prohibits calls to both cell phones and residential lines. Live calls and artificial or prerecorded voice messages and texts are prohibited.

If you are called after you place your name on the Do Not Call Registry, you may be able to sue for all calls, including the first one, if you receive two telemarketing calls within a 12-month period. Again, it does not matter if the calls are live, prerecorded, or robocalls and if they come to either your residence or your cell or if they come to you by text.

D. Credit Repair Organizations Act (CROA)

Credit Repair Organizations Act (CROA)
By Attorney Ronald C. Sykstus

The Credit Repair Organizations Act (CROA) is a federal consumer law found among the other various federal consumer protection laws and is located at 15 U.S.C. 1679. This law was enacted by Congress in 1996 in response to the trend of credit repair companies using deceitful practices to take advantage of debtors looking to improve their credit scores. The purpose of the statute is to ensure that the public is provided with information necessary to make an informed decision regarding the purchase of credit repair services and to protect the public from unfair deceptive advertising and business practices.

A credit repair organization (CRO) is defined as any person who uses any instrumentality of interstate commerce or the mail to sell, provide, perform, or represent that such person can or will sell or provide or perform any services for the express or implied purpose of improving any consumer's credit record, credit history, or credit rating or providing advice or assistance to a consumer with regard to any activity service like this in return for the payment of money or other valuable consideration. This definition of credit repair organizations does not include nonprofit organizations. The Act is not limited to just credit repair organizations but also to any person who makes any statement or counsel and advice to any consumer which is untrue or misleading with respect to any consumer's credit worthiness, credit standing, or credit capacity to any credit reporting agency or to any person who extends credit to the consumer.

Of utmost importance, the Act provides that **no** credit report or organization may charge or receive any money or other valuable consideration for the performance of any service which its CRO has agreed to perform **before** such services are fully performed. What that means is **a credit repair organization cannot take any money up front, and no advance payment is allowed before the actual service is performed.** Additionally, this law provides that a written contract is required and that the terms and conditions of payment, including the total amount of all payments, detailed description of services to be performed, estimate or date by which the services will be completed, the credit report organizations will named principal business address in the notice of right to cancel involved near the signature line. Contracts that fail to comply with this act are void and unenforceable. Additionally, the consumer must be given a copy of all documents at the time of signing, and any waiver of any protection or any right provided under CROA is void and unenforceable, and any attempt to obtain a waiver is a violation of the act as well.

Any consumer who is damaged by a violation of this act is entitled to actual damages and punitive damages along with attorney's fees and costs. There is a five-year statute of limitations from the date of the violation.

CROA is a strong law, and it endeavors to protect consumers from paying upfront money for any type of credit repair or credit report improvement. Consumers should be aware of their rights under this act and under the Fair Credit Reporting Act (FCRA).

E. Electronic Funds Transfer Act (EFTA)

What Can I Do If a Debt Collector or Creditor Is Taking Money From My Bank Account and I Want It to Stop? (The Electronic Funds Transfer Act, or EFTA, Is the Federal Law That Deals with This Issue)

By Attorney Ronald C Sykstus

Many times creditors and debt collectors will coerce, usually by harassment, people into allowing them to take money directly from their checking or savings bank accounts. You have an absolute right to stop this seizure of your money at any time. Additionally, prior to doing so, the creditor or debt collector must issue written notification to you of the intent to take money from your bank account at least five days prior to the transaction where the money is taken. The law that applies here is called the Electronic Funds Transfer Act. The specific citation for this law is found under the grouping of federal consumer protection laws and is located at 15 U.S.C.§1601.

If a creditor or debt collector is taking money from your bank account and you want to stop the seizure of money, please notify your bank and tell them to issue a stop payment on it. Your bank will probably charge you $20 to $30 to do so. The second thing you must do is to write the creditor or debt collector a letter that says that they are no longer allowed to take any money from your bank account located at (name of bank) under account number (bank account number). You can further say in this letter that you terminate any authorization for them to access any money from your bank account and that they should never touch your bank account again or take any money from you. Make sure you sign and date the letter and mail it to the creditor or debt collector by certified mail, return receipt requested, and keep a copy of what you mail. Secondly, as mentioned above, please keep the originals of all letters you get from any creditor or debt collector who says that they are taking money from your bank account. Oftentimes, they will not mail this letter to you, and this violates the Electronic Funds Transfer Act. We are seeing this repeatedly now, especially with payday lenders and cash loan places, so it is very important to be aware of your rights. If your rights have been violated under this law, you may be able to sue the creditor or debt collector in federal court.

F. Fair Credit Billing Act (FCBA)

Fair Credit Billing Act (FCBA)
By Attorney Ronald C. Sykstus

The Fair Credit Billing Act (FCBA) is a subsection of the federal Truth in Lending Act (TILA). It is an important federal law for all consumers since it contains the billing error procedures at sections 1666 and 1666(a). These billing error procedures most commonly assist consumers when they are disputing credit card transactions on their credit card statements for which they do not believe they should be held liable. The billing error procedures under the FCBA are one option available to consumers. They are separate and apart from other dispute rights under TILA, such as protections for unauthorized use of a credit card and a credit card holder's right to assert claims and defenses against the credit card issuer. Failure to invoke the billing error procedures does not prevent a consumer from asserting these other protections but, in our view, it is always a good idea to assert FCBA rights for any transaction on a credit card billing statement that a consumer does not think is correctly his or hers.

To invoke the provisions of the FCBA, a consumer **must** submit a billing error notice **in writing** to the creditor no later than 60 days after the creditor first transmitted the first periodic statement that reflects the billing error. The 60-day period begins to run when the creditor first sends a statement to the consumer who alleges the billing error. As a result, we urge consumers to immediately review each and every credit card statement immediately upon receipt. If there is an error, then they must immediately dispute it in writing by identifying the transaction, the transaction date, who the listed creditor is, the account number, the amount, and any other identifying information. The consumer also needs to make sure that he or she clearly identifies himself or herself in the dispute. **The dispute should be in writing, signed and dated and mailed by certified mail, return receipt, to insure that the consumer can prove receipt of the billing dispute.** The dispute should be mailed directly to the credit card billing statement, and a copy should also be mailed to the merchant that is showing the error. We urge consumers to keep copies of all of these documents and proof of receipts of the signed green card from the postal service. If the error is not corrected, then the consumer may pursue remedies under the law.

In sum, consumers should immediately review all credit card billing statements to make sure they are correct. If there is an erroneous entry or charge on the credit card billing statement, it must be disputed immediately in writing—proof of receipt of the dispute is critical—and it must be done no later than 60 days from the date of the statement, though our strong recommendation is to dispute an erroneous credit charge immediately.

CHAPTER 20

CONCLUSION

We hope that you have found this information helpful and useful. At a minimum, this should serve as a starting point for any question you have about delinquent or problem debts, what can happen with them, and what you can do about them. As stated at the beginning of this book, we try our best to follow the golden rule and treat people as we want to be treated ourselves. If you need our assistance, please do not hesitate to contact us. Our offices are located in Alabama, Mississippi, and Tennessee. www.bondandbotes.com

11 U.S.C. § 101 et seq. requires that we say, "We are a debt relief agency and attorneys at law. We can help people file for bankruptcy relief, where appropriate, under the Bankruptcy Code."

This book and material are for general informational purposes only and are not meant to provide specific legal advice. The purchase and review of this book do not create an attorney-client relationship with any of the Bond and Botes lawyers or affiliated law offices. For that relationship to be created, our lawyers and law offices require a sit-down, face-to-face meeting and then a written and signed retainer agreement before we will act as your attorneys on your specific situation or legal matter. Our lawyers can only represent individuals in the states in which they are licensed to practice law, and presently we do not represent or counsel with prospective bankruptcy clients outside of the states of Alabama, Mississippi, and Tennessee.

CPSIA information can be obtained
at www.ICGtesting.com
Printed in the USA
LVHW05s0918010918
588583LV00004B/4/P

9 781457 536212